LEARN HORSEBACK RIDING IN A WEEKEND

LEARN HORSEBACK RIDING IN A WEEKEND

MARY GORDON WATSON

Photography by Peter Chadwick

ALFRED A. KNOPF
New York
1998

A DORLING KINDERSLEY BOOK

This is a Borzoi Book published in 1998
by Alfred A. Knopf, Inc., by arrangement
with Dorling Kindersley

Art Editor Amanda Lunn
Project Editor Jo Weeks
Production Controller Deborah Wehner
Senior Art Editor Tina Vaughan
Managing Editor Sean Moore

Library of Congress Cataloging-in-Publication Data
Gordon Watson, Mary.
 Learn horseback riding in a weekend / Mary Gordon Watson ;
photography by Peter Chadwick. -- 1st American ed.
  p.   cm.
 "A Dorling Kindersley book."
 Includes index.
 ISBN 0-375-70302-0
 1. Horsemanship. I Title.
SF309 . G676 1992
798.2 ' 3--dc20   91-39210
                                                            CIP
Computer page make-up by Book Production Services
Reproduced by Colourscan, Singapore
Printed by KHL Printing Co Pte Ltd, Singapore

First American Edition Published 1992

First American Paperback Edition, June 1998

CONTENTS

INTRODUCTION

IT IS NEVER TOO LATE to start riding. It can be enjoyed at every level, by all ages – whether you prefer a gentle hack in the countryside, or want to do something more strenuous such as long distance trekking, jumping, or even competitive riding. Like most sports, it is more fun – and safer – if you learn the correct methods from the start. *Learn Horseback Riding in a Weekend* introduces you to riding for pleasure. The ultimate aim is to be in harmony with your horse, and while this is rarely completely achieved – even by the best riders – every step towards the goal will prove rewarding and make riding more enjoyable. This book doesn't pretend to make you into an expert in one weekend – that is impossible – but you should make a good start towards being a competent rider. I hope what follows helps you to avoid many of the pitfalls so that you get the most out of your riding and go on to enjoy it to the full.

Mary Gordon Watson

MARY GORDON WATSON

PREPARING FOR THE WEEKEND

Make your weekend a success with thorough preparation

YOUR ENJOYMENT OF RIDING, and future as a rider, depends on learning the correct methods right from the beginning. Seek expert advice to help you choose the best riding school, with suitable horses and a good instructor. It is also a good idea to take advice on what you need to wear, to be both comfortable and safe on a horse. If you have ridden before, be prepared to start completely afresh, as you may have acquired bad habits that will affect your progress. Part of the fascination of riding is that you never finish learning. Every horse varies in ability and character; you will learn something new from each one. The

RIDING GEAR
The most important items are your hard hat, or skull cap, which must fit perfectly, and safe footwear (see pp.16-17).

Gloves

Saddle

Rubber snaffle

TACK
You do not need to own any tack at this stage. However, you should know the parts of the saddle and bridle, as well as the bits worn by a horse, and understand their various roles, how they work, and how to fit them correctly (see pp.14-15).

Loose ring snaffle   *Egg-butt snaffle*

Pelham

Appaloosa

weekend is only the start. But a good start, based on sound foundations, will make it possible for you to become a confident, effective, and happy rider. Spend every spare moment getting to know horses better – how they look, move, and behave. You can learn by watching others being taught, and by studying experienced riders, whether they are practicing at home, or are in a competition. You need to be in at least average physical condition to enjoy riding, so it is recommended that you do some of the exercises on pp.24-25 beforehand to improve your fitness and co-ordination. Throughout this book you will find riding terms in **bold**; they are given further explanation in the glossary (pp.92-93).

Horse and rider are well suited

Bicycling

Trunk twists

EXERCISE
The fitter you are, the easier it will be to learn to ride well without suffering from aching muscles, stiffness, and fatigue. If your body is in very "soft" condition, build up your stamina, flexibility, and resilience by doing some suitable exercises (see pp.24-25).

RIDING SCHOOL
Find a school where the horses, stables, equipment, and facilities are in good condition (see pp.18-19). Look for high standards.

INSTRUCTOR
Choose an experienced instructor who inspires confidence and makes riding fun (see pp.20-21).

Paces

KNOW YOUR HORSE

Learning to identify your horse's physical characteristics

IT IS USEFUL TO KNOW what the different parts of your horse are called when you are learning to handle, groom, and tack up, and when you are riding under instruction. Understanding how he works is essential for good riding. Much of his athletic ability depends on correct **conformation**, he must be built to carry a rider's weight with ease. Markings and colors distinguish one horse from another, while different breeds have individual characteristics.

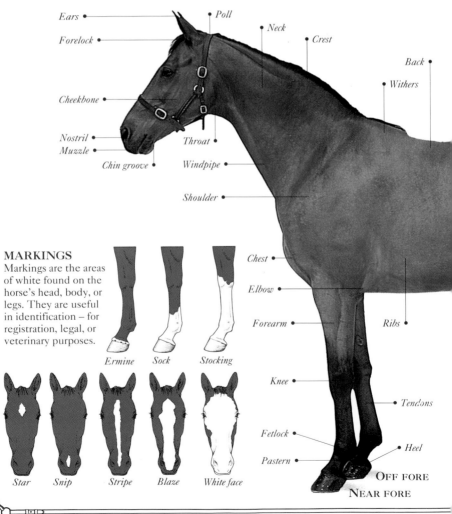

Ears • *Poll* • *Neck* • *Crest* • *Back* • *Withers*

Forelock •

Cheekbone •

Nostril • *Throat* •
Muzzle •
Chin groove • *Windpipe* •

Shoulder •

MARKINGS
Markings are the areas of white found on the horse's head, body, or legs. They are useful in identification – for registration, legal, or veterinary purposes.

Chest •
Elbow •
Forearm •
Ribs •

Ermine   *Sock*   *Stocking*

Knee •

Tendons •

Fetlock •

Heel •

Pastern •

Star   *Snip*   *Stripe*   *Blaze*   *White face*

OFF FORE

NEAR FORE

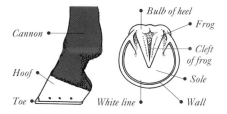

Cannon

Bulb of heel

Frog

Cleft of frog

Hoof

Sole

Toe

White line

Wall

THE FOOT

The hard exterior wall of the foot encases an intricate structure, which must be looked after properly. Roads and rough surfaces, combined with carrying weight, make it necessary to fit shoes to protect the foot. The hoof grows continuously and the shoes may wear thin, so horses need re-shoeing about every four weeks.

COLOR

There is a wide range of coat color, making each horse unique. For instance, a bay can range from dark mahogany to a pale, sandy shade. The color will often differ from winter to summer, too. Bays, browns, and duns have black points – the tips of the ears, the mane and tail, and the legs from below the knees and hocks. Chestnuts and grays have points in different shades of the same color.

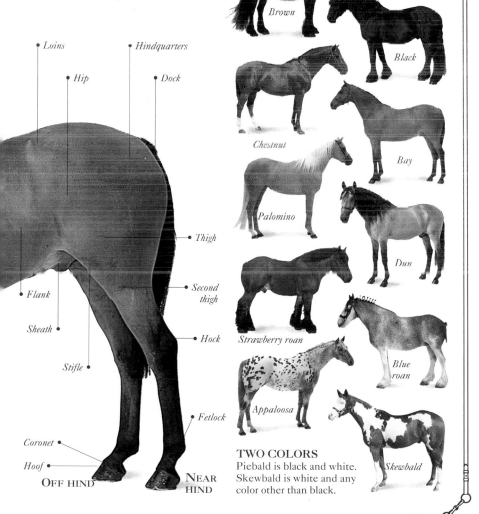

Loins

Hindquarters

Hip

Dock

Thigh

Second thigh

Flank

Sheath

Hock

Stifle

Fetlock

Coronet

Hoof

OFF HIND

NEAR HIND

Gray

Brown

Black

Chestnut

Bay

Palomino

Dun

Strawberry roan

Blue roan

Appaloosa

Skewbald

TWO COLORS

Piebald is black and white. Skewbald is white and any color other than black.

THE GAITS

The horse's action, which alters as he changes speed

A HORSE HAS FOUR BASIC GAITS – walk, trot, canter, and gallop. He walks at about 8km/h (3mph), and can gallop at up to 72km/h (44mph). He can reverse (rein back), turn on the spot, and move sideways (laterally). A well-balanced, supple horse can be trained to produce variations on the basic **working** gaits. **Collected** gaits have shorter, slightly **elevated** strides. **Medium** gaits show lengthened strides, while in **extended** gaits, each step covers a maximum distance.

THE GALLOP

The gallop is the fastest, most **extended** gait. Like the canter, the near fore leg **leads** when going left-handed, the off fore when going right-handed but, unlike the canter, the gallop has four foot falls. To gallop safely, a smooth, yielding stretch of ground is needed, and the horse must be fit. Only a competent rider should gallop.

THE WALK

The walk has four even foot falls (four-beat). Each stride is of equal length. At least two feet are on the ground at the same time. Sequence: near hind, near fore, off hind, off fore.

THE HORSE AT WALK
At the walk, the horse "tracks up". This means that the print of his hind foot overlaps that left by the fore foot on the same side.

THE RIDER •
The rider sits upright over the center of balance. Supple shoulders, elbows, and wrists allow the arms to follow the movement.

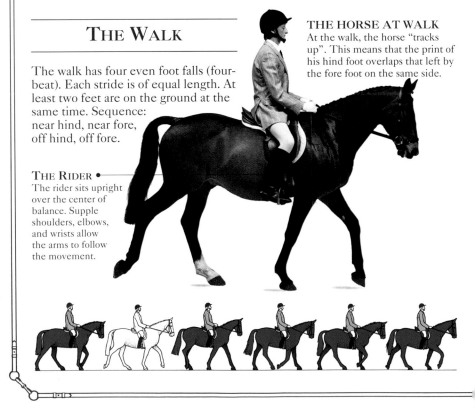

THE TROT

The trot is a two-beat gait. The legs move in diagonal pairs, separated by a moment of **suspension**. Sequence: off fore and near hind, near fore and off hind.

THE RIDER •
The rider can either rise or sit in the saddle. Here, he sits on the left diagonal – the near fore and off hind are on the ground – and will rise as these feet leave the ground.

THE CANTER

THE HORSE AT CANTER
This horse is cantering to the right, with off fore and off hind legs **leading**. It is on the wrong lead if it goes left with off legs leading, or right with near legs leading.

The canter has a three-beat rhythm, with a moment when all four feet are in the air. Sequence for canter to the right: near hind, off hind and near fore, off fore. In left canter the opposite happens.

THE RIDER •
The rider sits upright in the saddle as his body and hands follow the slightly rocking motion of the canter.

THE TACK

The saddle, bridle, and other equipment used for riding a horse

ALL RIDERS SHOULD KNOW how tack works and how to fit it correctly. If the tack is the wrong type, does not fit, or is in bad condition, the horse will be uncomfortable. An appropriate saddle adds to your comfort and progress. It enables you to sit correctly and distributes your weight evenly on either side of the horse's spine. The bridle should be made of good-quality leather and should be kept clean and supple. Bits come in different shapes and sizes and act with varying degrees of influence on the horse's mouth.

HEAD PIECE •
This adjusts the bit's height.

BROWBAND •
Stops the bridle slipping back.

CHEEK PIECE •
Attaches the head piece to the bit.

THROAT-LATCH •
Prevents bridle slipping forward.

NOSEBAND •
Helps to stop the horse avoiding the bit.

BIT •
An egg-butt snaffle with smooth side joints to avoid chafing.

REINS •
Reins can be leather, often with rubber grips, or nylon webbing. Very thick reins are unwieldy and insensitive, long ones are dangerous.

THE BRIDLE

The bridle consists of adjustable lengths of leather, buckled together to form a harness that holds the bit in the horse's mouth at the correct height. The reins are attached to the bit.

Jointed, rubber snaffle   *Straight-bar, nylon snaffle*

Loose-ring German snaffle   *Egg-butt snaffle*

Pelham with roundings

SIMPLE BITS
Usually, the most suitable bit is a snaffle. A thin mouthpiece is generally more severe than a thick one. Rubber mouthpieces are mildest. The pelham is for less sensitive mouths and combines the action of snaffle and **curb**. It has two reins, to vary its effect, but roundings can be fitted to allow the use of a single rein.

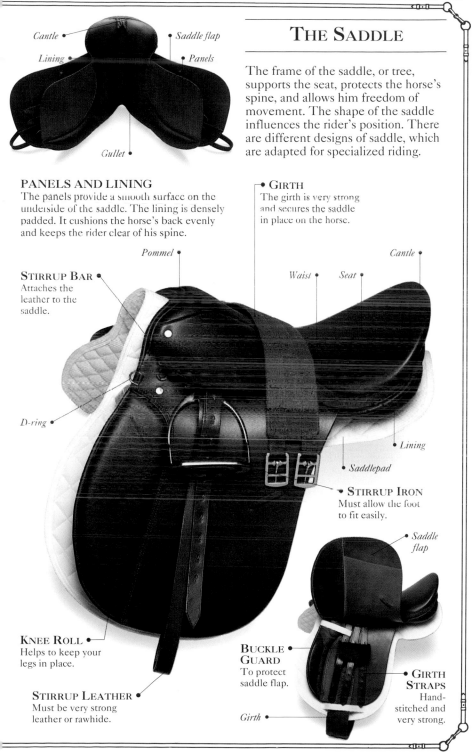

Cantle •   • *Saddle flap*

Lining •   • *Panels*

Gullet •

THE SADDLE

The frame of the saddle, or tree, supports the seat, protects the horse's spine, and allows him freedom of movement. The shape of the saddle influences the rider's position. There are different designs of saddle, which are adapted for specialized riding.

PANELS AND LINING
The panels provide a smooth surface on the underside of the saddle. The lining is densely padded. It cushions the horse's back evenly and keeps the rider clear of his spine.

• GIRTH
The girth is very strong and secures the saddle in place on the horse.

Pommel •

Waist   *Seat* •

Cantle •

STIRRUP BAR •
Attaches the leather to the saddle.

D-ring •

Lining

Saddlepad •

• STIRRUP IRON
Must allow the foot to fit easily.

• *Saddle flap*

KNEE ROLL •
Helps to keep your legs in place.

STIRRUP LEATHER •
Must be very strong leather or rawhide.

BUCKLE GUARD •
To protect saddle flap.

Girth •

• GIRTH STRAPS
Hand-stitched and very strong.

RIDING GEAR

Clothes and equipment designed to make riding easier, safer, and more comfortable

THE MOST IMPORTANT ITEM of riding gear is your hat. Don't wear one that is sub-standard, does not fit perfectly, or has a fixed peak which, on impact, could cause concussion or a broken nose. Strong footwear is essential. Boots or shoes must have pronounced heels to prevent them sliding through the irons. They must not have half-soles, or buckles that could trap your foot in the stirrup. Tennis shoes and soft shoes don't provide enough protection. If you have long hair, tie it up or put it in a hairnet. Don't wear loose or noisy garments, dangling jewelry or scarves – they can frighten the horses.

Wool

Cotton

Leather

GLOVES
To avoid chafing from the reins, always wear gloves, which also keep the hands clean. They must fit closely, for a sensitive feel on the reins and a firm hold when wet.

FORMAL WEAR

Formal clothes are worn for competitions and special occasions. They look smart and are practical. A dark blue or black jacket or a tweed hacking jacket is worn over a pale shirt. With a dark jacket, a tie, or a white or cream stock, and a tie-pin are worn. A patterned or colored stock is worn with the hacking jacket. The tie-pin is fastened horizontally for safety. This formal outfit is completed with a hard hat, which has a black or navy cover; breeches, which can be beige, cream, or yellow; black boots, made from leather or synthetic material; and gloves. Spurs and a whip are optional additions for experienced riders.

Stock
Black jacket
Hacking jacket

COMPETITORS
These competitors for a showing class wear tweed hacking jackets with pale breeches, boots, and blunt spurs. Their bowler hats are traditional headgear but are not considered adequate protection for everyday riding.

HEADS FIRST

Both the skull cap, or crash helmet, and the lighter, less solid hard hat must be fitted with a safety harness, for keeping them on, and be an approved standard version. A skull cap gives the best protection. A cover with a brim shields the eyes from rain or sun.

Skull cap

Hard hat

INFORMAL WEAR

The correct hat and boots are essential. Dark breeches, riding trousers, or close fitting jeans are useful for casual riding. It is best to wear a long-sleeved top to protect your arms.

PADDED JACKET •
In the event of a fall, a lightweight, padded jacket will absorb some of the impact and soften your landing.

SWEATER •
A fitted sweater gives a clear outline so your teacher can correct your position and see signs of tension easily.

• **BREECHES**
Breeches fit to just below the calf. Areas in contact with the saddle fit smoothly, with no creases or seams to cause discomfort.

JODHPURS •
Jodhpurs extend to the ankles and, like breeches, have "strappings", or reinforcements along the inside leg.

BOOTS •
Long boots protect your legs, and should fit closely for comfort and support. Rubber ones are economical and easy to clean, but leather boots are stronger and do not "sweat" inside.

JODHPUR BOOTS •
Elastic-sided jodhpur boots with a well-defined heel are safer than shoes as they protect the ankle and will not slide through the stirrup.

THE RIDING SCHOOL

What to look for in a suitable riding school

LOOK FOR A SCHOOL that is recommended by experts and provides high standards of instruction and **horsemanship** from experienced, qualified teachers. It should have a pleasant atmosphere, a well-organized routine, and willing, healthy horses with well-shod feet. A covered, or enclosed arena is ideal, but well-kept facilities, however unimpressive, are preferable to a neglected school where the riding area is rutted, or littered with broken jumps. Check that the stables and the feed shed are clean, that the tack is in good condition, and that the hay is good quality. A telephone, and provisions for first aid and fire are also important.

MUCK HEAP
The muck heap is handy for the stables and disposal vehicles, but is out of sight, to avoid the smell and flies.

TACK ROOM
The tack is kept in a dry dust-free room with space for cleaning it and for other gear, like stable blankets.

FIRE STATION

A fire extinguisher and hose pipe are essential precautions, and the "NO SMOKING" rule must be strictly enforced.

STABLING

The stables are ventilated, dry, well-drained, and clean. A **loose box** should be about 4m (12ft) square.

FIELDS

The fields are not bare, weedy, or worm-infested. They have fresh water, good drainage, and safe fences.

INDOOR SCHOOL

An indoor school provides safe conditions with no distractions and can be used in all weathers, at any time of day or, if lit, night.

THE INSTRUCTOR

Good, sound instruction is as vital to learning to ride as a suitable horse

YOUR LESSONS SHOULD PROVIDE you with the secure foundations for becoming a confident rider. A good teacher will ensure you are always prepared, happy, and safe, and will instill in you a respect for your horse. Your instructor should be enthusiastic and must enjoy working with people and horses. Self-confidence and an ability to communicate are essential, as are patience and tact. Always ready to encourage, a good instructor should give only constructive criticism. Other qualities you should look for are: keen observation, a clear, carrying voice, which is interesting and easy to listen to, and an ability to deliver simple instructions and explanations and to establish a rapport with each pupil.

GIVING A LESSON

Each lesson must have a plan and goal, and should make the best use of the time. Your instructor should be punctual and well turned out.

CLOTHES •
The instructor wears riding gear so that she can get on the horse to demonstrate, or to correct a fault.

POSITION •
Teaching from the ground is safer and more practical, and it enables the instructor to make adjustments to tack or position.

WAIT YOUR TURN
Periods of rest during a lesson allow you to relax and give your horse a refreshing break, but be attentive as you wait for your turn.

PERSONAL HELP
Expect to receive personal attention and always feel able to discuss your problems and how to deal with them.

TYPES OF LESSON

IN A CLASS OR GROUP
Group lessons, in an enclosed area, are ideal for up to six riders of similar standard. Helpers are normally present to lead if necessary, and a competent rider or a free-going horse is chosen as leader.

ON A LEADING REIN
Being led often helps a nervous rider to gain confidence, or controls a naughty horse, but it is rarely the most satisfactory way to learn since the pace is limited and the instructor's view of the rider's position is obscured by the person leading.

ON THE GROUND
Off the horse, you can learn about stable management, grooming, feeding, fitting tack, tacking up, road safety, and first aid. Advanced riding techniques can also be studied.

ON THE LUNGE
When on the lunge, the instructor controls the horse, while the rider concentrates on improving balance and developing a strong seat and legs. The rider does not have reins but a **neckstrap** is used for safety.

• POSTURE
Even when still, maintain the correct position so that it becomes habitual. This rider has let her hands rest on her horse.

• ASSISTED MOUNTING
An instructor's assistant holds the horse and the opposite stirrup leather while the rider is taught how to get on and off correctly.

CONCENTRATION
Concentration is difficult to maintain and will need to be stimulated during the lesson. The emphasis should be balanced between the physical and mental effort, and relaxation.

THE ASSISTANT'S ROLE
If mounted, the assistant can act as the leader or demonstrate a skill. If on foot, she can avert possible mishaps, or lead a rider in difficulty.

THE HORSE

Choosing the right horse to be your teacher

ASK THE ADVICE OF an experienced horseman or instructor when you select the horse on which you learn to ride. It is true that "good horses make good riders", but beware of the advanced, highly trained, or very sensitive horse. This sort of horse is unlikely to suit a beginner, whose balance and position in the saddle, and mastery of the **aids,** are not well-established. Any involuntary or clumsy movement could confuse and upset him, thus provoking a reaction that might lead to loss of control and a possible accident situation. A horse of suitable size that has had sound basic training, is ideal. For a new rider to develop that all-important confidence, it is also essential that the horse has a willing yet quiet temperament and he must also be experienced with beginners.

THE RIGHT FIT

A small, light rider on a large horse (near left) will find it difficult to give the correct **aids** for effective control. If the rider is too tall, so that his feet dangle down away from the horse's body (far left), or is too heavy, this can affect the horse's **action** or balance.

AN UNSUITABLE HORSE

HE IS IN POOR CONDITION
He looks tired and has a dull coat and eyes. He looks listless – a sign of overwork or boredom. He is too fat, or he is thin and weak. His feet are long or cracked, or his shoes are over-worn. He has **girth galls,** or **saddle sores.** There is heat or swelling in his legs or joints. He has a thick discharge from the nose.

Saddle sore

HE IS BADLY BEHAVED
He is temperamental or restless – typical signs of a restless horse are: he does not stand still for mounting, he looks about nervously, he is excitable in company with others – jogging, **shying,** or **bucking.** He dislikes or is frightened by other horses and threatens to kick or bite them. He does not slow down or stop when he is asked to, or he is difficult to turn. He refuses to go any faster, despite the rider's kicks. He is **nappy** and tries to stop or veers towards his stable or the exit to the manège, or he refuses to leave the other horses. Worst of all – he **rears.**

A SUITABLE HORSE

These horses look alert, yet calm. The larger, bay horse is built to carry up to 82.5kg (180 lbs) with ease, while the smaller, palomino horse is suitable for a light person up to about 57kg (125 lbs).

GOOD CONDITION
These horses are in good condition for the work required, being neither too fat nor too thin. They appear healthy and well cared for.

SADDLES
These are general purpose saddles, with saddlepads fitted for comfort and to absorb sweat. The stirrups have rubber insets for grip.

BRIDLE
This bridle has a simple snaffle bit. The bridle fits correctly and is clean and in a safe condition.

APPROPRIATE SIZE
A horse's ability to carry weight depends on his height and build. A correct **conformation** (see pp.10-11) makes him stronger.

HE WEARS UNSUITABLE TACK
His tack is dirty, with cracked leather and broken stitching. Complicated bits or other gadgets suggest he is not a novice ride.

SEVERE BITS
Thin bits in the wrong hands cause pain and can do more harm than good.

Kimblewick

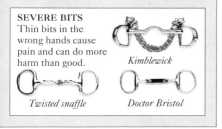

Twisted snaffle

Doctor Bristol

CHARACTER
There are many types of horse and pony that are particularly suitable for beginners. Sound training is necessary, but a placid, co-operative nature and smooth paces are more important for the beginner than a horse's ability (a brilliant performer usually needs an experienced rider).

FIT FOR RIDING

Improving your fitness, strength, suppleness, and stamina to make riding easier

YOU DON'T NEED enormous physical strength to be a good rider, but being reasonably fit does help. Neither you nor your horse will be comfortable if you are tired, aching, or out of breath. These exercises will improve your general fitness, and develop your balance and co-ordination. Riding is more enjoyable, and progress quicker, if you can avoid making involuntary movements with your arms, hands, or legs, which could upset or be misunderstood by your horse.

SUPPLENESS

Do these exercises to loosen the joints at the neck, shoulders, elbows, wrists, hips, knees, and ankles. They will also improve muscular suppleness and release tension, which is tiring and might also make the horse tense.

LEG SWINGING
Bending the knee very slightly, swing your left leg back and forth about ten times. Repeat with your right leg. Support yourself with a chair back or something similar, if necessary.

SIDE FLEXING
Stand straight, with feet apart and arms outstretched, at shoulder height. Keeping your arms straight, stretch your right side by reaching down your left side as far as you can. Repeat this stretch on both sides, as many times as you can.

TRUNK TWISTS
In the same position as for side flexing, swing your arms as far around as you can, twisting your body. Then swing back the other way.

FITNESS

Exercises that improve lung fitness will prove useful for riding. Gradually build up your stamina by increasing the number of repeats. Be careful if you are elderly or very unfit – some of these exercises are strenuous if done too often or too quickly.

JUMPING ROPE

Jumping rope is ideal for building up stamina. Time yourself, doing as many jumps as you can before getting out of breath.

SQUATS

Crouch on your heels, with arms by your side. Spring up, stretching your arms above your head. Repeat as many times as you can.

STRENGTH

If you are unfit, your muscles will need strengthening and toning to provide better support in the saddle, and to enable you to ride for longer. Do exercises that stretch and contract the muscles, particularly those in your legs.

STEP-UPS

Put your left foot on a step, spring up, so that both legs are together, then lower the right foot to the ground. Repeat ten times with each leg.

BICYCLING

Lie on your back with your hands by your sides or supporting the arch of your back. Raise your legs and bottom upwards and bicycle in the air.

SIT-UPS

Lie on your back with knees bent and feet flat. Sit up, without using your arms, then lie down again. Start with five repeats.

THE WEEKEND COURSE

Understanding the course at a glance

———————•———————

THE COURSE COVERS ten basic skills in two days. On the first day, the important preliminary skills are learned. You learn how to approach your horse, catch him, and get him ready to be ridden, and you spend time in the saddle, making adjustments so that you are ready to move off. On the second day you can progress to the more advanced skills of trotting, lunging exercises to improve balance, and, if you are very confident, cantering. You may find two days' riding a little tiring – you will certainly find muscles you never knew you had! So, although this course can be done over one weekend, you might like to take it at an easier pace. After all, the idea is to enjoy yourself.

DAY 1			Hours	Page
Skill 1	Horse sense		1/2	28-29
Skill 2	Preparing to ride		1	30-33
Skill 3	Tacking up		1/2	34-37
Skill 4	Mounting		1/2	38-41
Skill 5	In the saddle		1/2	42-49
Skill 6	First steps		1	50-55

Picking up feet

Quick-release knot

Grooming tools

Leading your horse

Exercises in the saddle

CLOCKS
A small clock appears on the first page of each new skill. It indicates how long you might spend on that skill and where it fits into the day. For example, look at the clock on p.30. The blue segment covers 1 hour and shows the time set aside for Skill 2: Preparing to Ride; the gray shaded segment shows you have already spent half an hour learning Skill 1: Horse Sense.

RATING SYSTEM •••••
Each skill in this book is rated according to its degree of difficulty. One bullet (•) denotes that the skill is comparatively easy. Five bullets (•••••) indicate it is more challenging and, indeed, you may not be able to master it in one weekend.

GHOSTED IMAGES
The paler images in some sequences are steps that are then described in detail.

Turning as a ride

Cantering

DAY 2		Hours	Page
Skill 7	Trotting	½	56-59
Skill 8	Lessons on the lunge	1½	60-63
Skill 9	Group riding	1½	64-67
Skill 10	Cantering	½	68-71

Series of loops

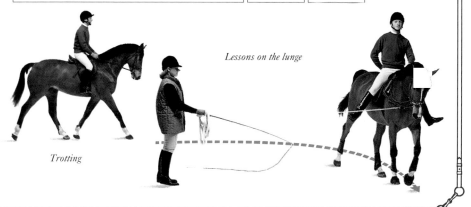

Lessons on the lunge

Trotting

1 HORSE SENSE

Definition: *Understanding the way your horse thinks and behaves*

LEARNING HOW TO BEHAVE when with your horse is the first step towards building a good working relationship with him. A well-treated horse is trusting but a frightened horse can be very strong and could be dangerously unsafe. Always speak calmly. Horses are sensitive to tone of voice, so never shout. Avoid noises like road drills or motor bikes. Don't move suddenly or carelessly when around horses. Use persuasion to encourage your horse. Horses never forget a bad experience, but you can use their memory to your advantage as they will also remember praise and rewards. Horses work best when they are in a happy environment and they like routine.

OBJECTIVE: To learn to communicate with horses, move around them safely, and handle them confidently. *Rating* •••••

• **AT EASE**
A relaxed horse who is used to being handled.

BE AWARE

However quiet he seems, never take your horse for granted. Any strange sights, sounds, or actions could startle him and he might kick you or break loose. Always speak calmly, warning him where you are and telling him what you are going to do. Handle him gently and avoid sudden movements.

• **YOUR POSITION**
Never leave yourself vulnerable to being stepped on. When picking up his feet, bend down and be ready to move away quickly if necessary.

• **INSPECTING A HIND FOOT**
Facing the rear, put your hand on his quarters, run it down the back of his leg to his hock, then the inside of the lower leg. Say, "up". Squeeze the joint gently if he resists.

MAKING CONTACT

Approach calmly, speaking with a quiet voice. Let him see you. Use your touch and tone of voice to soothe, encourage, or guide him. Don't rush.

WATCH HIS EARS •
The ears can tell you much about his mood. Ears back suggests discontent or awareness of something behind. Flattened-back ears denote anger. Ears pricked forward means he is attentive, willing, and bold.

• WALKING BEHIND
Always warn a horse before you go behind him. Run your hand over his back and quarters as you move to the rear, so that he knows where you are.

• TICKLISH AREAS
When handling your horse, be wary of touching ticklish areas like his flanks, stomach, and inside thighs.

HOW TO FEED
To avoid accidental nips, offer tidbits, like apples, sugar lumps, or carrots, with your hand flat, fingers together.

BEHAVIOR AND TEMPERAMENT

INTERPRETING HIS MOOD
It is very important to be able to anticipate mood and recognize how your horse may react in different circumstances. A very fresh and excited horse may jog and pull, or even **buck**, and he may need an experienced rider to calm him down. If your horse is reluctant to leave his companions he may be obstinate or lazy and need strong riding. Sweating, along with raised heart and breathing rates (not caused by heat or exertion), may be due to pain or fear and should not be ignored. Other signs of apprehension are snorting, or showing the whites of the eyes.

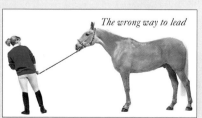

The wrong way to lead

PERSUASION IS BEST
Use persuasion, not force. If he refuses to be led, get someone to urge him from behind, or use a long whip to tap his quarters or ribs.

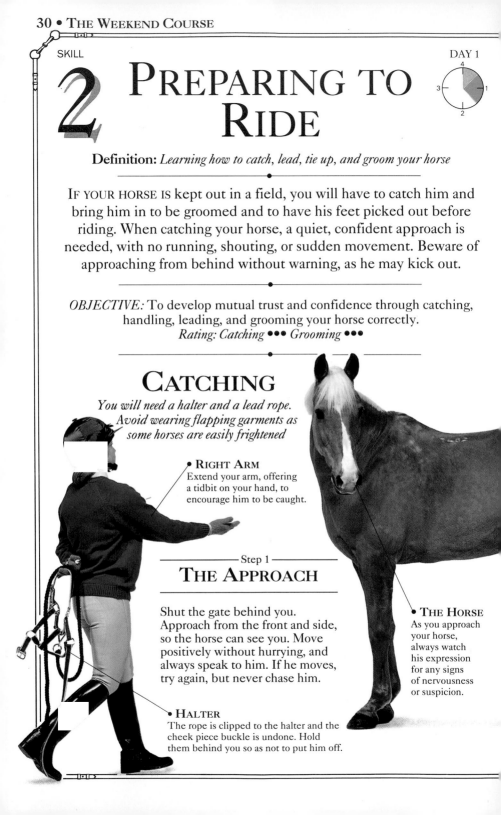

SKILL

DAY 1

2 PREPARING TO RIDE

Definition: *Learning how to catch, lead, tie up, and groom your horse*

IF YOUR HORSE IS kept out in a field, you will have to catch him and bring him in to be groomed and to have his feet picked out before riding. When catching your horse, a quiet, confident approach is needed, with no running, shouting, or sudden movement. Beware of approaching from behind without warning, as he may kick out.

OBJECTIVE: To develop mutual trust and confidence through catching, handling, leading, and grooming your horse correctly.
Rating: Catching ••• *Grooming* •••

CATCHING

You will need a halter and a lead rope. Avoid wearing flapping garments as some horses are easily frightened

• **RIGHT ARM**
Extend your arm, offering a tidbit on your hand, to encourage him to be caught.

——— Step 1 ———
THE APPROACH

Shut the gate behind you. Approach from the front and side, so the horse can see you. Move positively without hurrying, and always speak to him. If he moves, try again, but never chase him.

• **THE HORSE**
As you approach your horse, always watch his expression for any signs of nervousness or suspicion.

• **HALTER**
The rope is clipped to the halter and the cheek piece buckle is undone. Hold them behind you so as not to put him off.

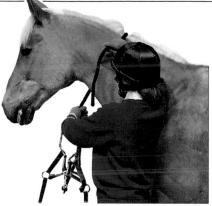 

2. CATCHING HIM

While he is munching the tidbit, slip the free end of the lead rope around his neck, close to his head, and hold the ends together securely while you prepare to put on the halter.

3. FITTING THE HALTER

Put the noseband over his muzzle and, reaching below his throat and behind his head, flick the head piece up over his head, behind the ears, buckling it on the near side.

WALKING QUIETLY •
Your horse should follow quietly, but stay alert in case he is startled and pulls away.

—— Step 4 ——
LEADING

Say "walk on", or give a click of the tongue, and start to walk, giving a slight jerk on the rope if necessary. Look ahead, and the horse should follow your lead.

• **POSITION**
Walk level with the horse's shoulder for maximum control. Practice leading on both sides.

• **THE ROPE**
Hold the rope in both hands. Never twist it around a hand or tie it to yourself.

GROOMING

Your horse's coat, mane, and tail need to be brushed, and his feet need to be picked out to keep him clean and healthy

PICKING OUT FEET

Before grooming, tie up your horse with the quick-release knot shown below. Start by removing dirt and stones from his feet to keep them in a healthy condition. Pick out each foot in a regular sequence.

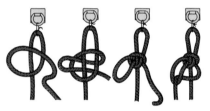

THE QUICK-RELEASE KNOT
Pass the lead rope through a loop of string attached to a wall ring. Secure it with the quick-release knot above. In an emergency, the knot is quickly undone. If the horse panics, the string breaks, preventing injury.

HEEL TO TOE •
Using a blunt-ended hoof pick, work from heel to toe. Avoid pressing on the frog.

Grooming tools and box

Using the dandy brush

GROOMING
The dandy brush (above) is used to remove mud and sweat marks from the body. Never use it on the mane or tail as it will damage them. Use brisk strokes, but avoid any tender areas like the head, and take care with clipped or thin-skinned horses. Starting near the head and working towards the tail, use the body brush (right) for deep grooming. Brush with firm, circular strokes in the same direction as the hair growth. Every few strokes, clean the brush with a curry comb.

Using the curry comb

SPONGING

It may be easier to remove the halter to clean his head. First, use the body brush; then, with a damp sponge, wipe the eyes, nostrils, and muzzle. Use a separate sponge to clean under his tail.

FOOT CARE •

The hooves are brushed with hoof oil. This helps to replace the natural oils and prevents the feet from becoming dry and brittle.

MANE AND TAIL

Use a body brush to groom your horse's mane and tail. Hold the tail to one side of his rear end, to avoid being kicked, and separate a few strands at a time, removing tangles or straw. After they have been brushed, lay the mane and tail in place with a dampened water brush. The tail may then be bandaged to keep it neatly in shape.

GROOMING TOOLS

Grooming tools include: body and dandy brushes, metal or rubber curry combs, a mane comb, a hoof pick, sponges to clean his face and dock, a water brush for laying the mane and tail, a stable rubber for a final polish, and the hoof oil and brush. A sweat scraper is useful for removing water after washing.

Sponges

Sweat scraper

Dandy brush

Curry combs

Stable rubber hoof oil & brush

Water brush

Hoof pick

Body brush

Mane comb

Tack box

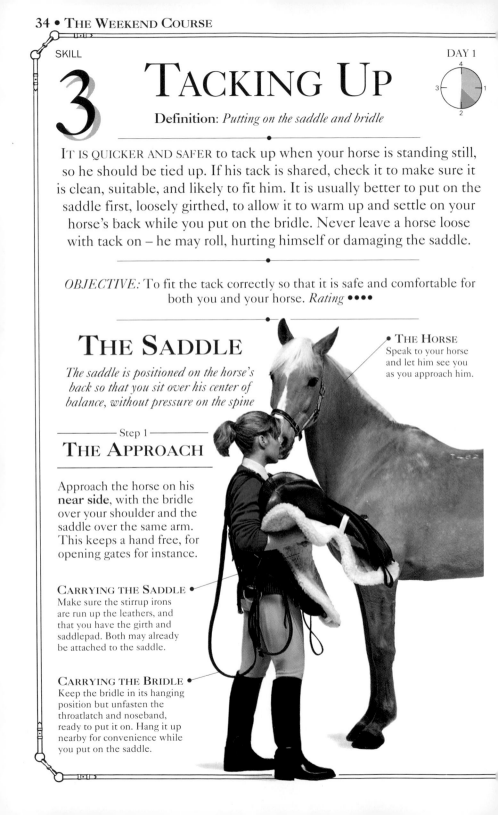

SKILL

3

TACKING UP

DAY 1

Definition: *Putting on the saddle and bridle*

IT IS QUICKER AND SAFER to tack up when your horse is standing still, so he should be tied up. If his tack is shared, check it to make sure it is clean, suitable, and likely to fit him. It is usually better to put on the saddle first, loosely girthed, to allow it to warm up and settle on your horse's back while you put on the bridle. Never leave a horse loose with tack on – he may roll, hurting himself or damaging the saddle.

OBJECTIVE: To fit the tack correctly so that it is safe and comfortable for both you and your horse. *Rating* ••••

THE SADDLE

The saddle is positioned on the horse's back so that you sit over his center of balance, without pressure on the spine

• THE HORSE
Speak to your horse and let him see you as you approach him.

——— Step 1 ———
THE APPROACH

Approach the horse on his **near side**, with the bridle over your shoulder and the saddle over the same arm. This keeps a hand free, for opening gates for instance.

CARRYING THE SADDLE •
Make sure the stirrup irons are run up the leathers, and that you have the girth and saddlepad. Both may already be attached to the saddle.

CARRYING THE BRIDLE •
Keep the bridle in its hanging position but unfasten the throatlatch and noseband, ready to put it on. Hang it up nearby for convenience while you put on the saddle.

Move in the direction of the hair

Slip the girth through the loop on the saddlepad

2. POSITIONING THE SADDLE

Using both hands, lift the saddle above the **withers** and gently move it into position by sliding it with the hair, never against it. Feel that the saddlepad is lying flat and secure it – if it slips or rucks up it will do more harm than good.

Make sure that the saddlepad is pulled up into the saddle arch to avoid pressure on the withers

3. FASTENING THE GIRTH

On the **off side**, check the saddlepad, then lift down the girth and position it flat and straight, just behind the horse's elbow. Return to his **near side** and reach under his belly for the girth. Tighten it gradually and evenly on both near and off side buckles.

Smooth the hair under the girth and make sure that the skin is not pinched or caught anywhere

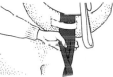

REMOVING THE SADDLE

Control your horse by looping the rein over your arm, or tie him up using a halter and rope. Always run up both stirrup irons when you dismount (see 1), this prevents them hitting your horse's sides if he moves off, and makes it easier for you to carry the saddle. As you slide the saddle off, be careful not to let it fall – if the tree breaks, the saddle will become useless.

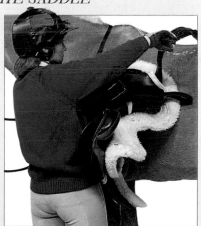

1. Slide the stirrup up the back part of the stirrup leather to the stirrup bar.

2. Resting the saddle flap on your wrist, ease the girth loose on the **near side**.

3. With one hand under the pommel, the other holding the cantle, lift the saddle and pull it towards you, then onto your lower arm. Fold the girth over the saddle.

SKILL
3

THE BRIDLE

Put on the bridle carefully. If you hurt the horse's mouth it may make him head-shy

• HIS HEAD
Hold both cheek pieces level and steady his head.

--- Step 1 ---
PLACING THE BIT

Take the bridle in the left hand, slip the halter off and put the reins over his head. Reach under his jaw, pass the bridle to the right hand, ease the bit into his mouth with the left hand, and raise the bridle to the ears.

OTHER METHOD
Below: Put your right arm between his ears to keep his head low while you place the bit in his mouth with your left hand.

HIS MOUTH •
Hold the bit on fingers and thumb, and gently press the gum at the gap between his teeth until he opens his mouth.

YOUR POSITION •
For maximum control, face forwards and stand alongside his neck, your shoulder in front of his.

THE FIT OF THE BIT

A correctly-fitted bit barely wrinkles the lips. A bit that is too narrow may pinch; if too low it may jangle against the teeth, and if too high it will rub and chafe the mouth. All these cause discomfort or pain, and may make the horse difficult to control.

Correct

Too high

Too low

Too wide

Too narrow

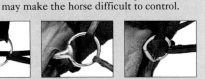

Secure your horse by putting the halter over the bridle and tying him up

2. FITTING THE BRIDLE

Keep the bit high in his mouth so that it cannot fall out again and, using both hands, slide the head piece over one ear, then the other. Pull his forelock over the browband. From the front, make sure the bit and bridle parts are level and adjust them to fit if necessary.

Use the width of your hand to check that the throatlatch will not restrict flexion or breathing

3. FASTENING THE BRIDLE

Buckle up the throatlatch, then fasten the noseband, checking it is midway between the cheekbone and bit. (The second strap on this **grakle noseband** is buckled in the chin groove.) Once he is tacked up, put a halter over the bridle and tie him up.

When leaving the horse tacked up, loop the reins under the stirrups so they are out of the way and cannot catch on anything

---

REMOVING THE BRIDLE

Make sure you have a halter close by or hanging on your arm before you remove the bridle. Bring the reins up the horse's neck so that they are closer to his head, in case you need them for control once you have removed the bridle.

Undo the noseband and throatlatch. Then, keeping his head still with one hand, slide the head piece over his ears with the other, easing the bit gently from his mouth. If he throws up his head and catches the bit on his teeth or his sensitive **bars**, it will hurt him and make him difficult to bridle next time. Hold the reins together, near his head, while you put on the halter then take them over his head.

After he has been out for a ride, your horse may feel sweaty and itchy and he will want to rub his bridle against anything available, so untack him immediately.

SKILL

4 MOUNTING

DAY 1

Definition: *Safe and practical ways of getting on – and off*

ALTHOUGH THERE ARE SEVERAL different ways to get on to a horse, all riders should be able to mount using the stirrup. Before mounting, make sure the saddle is in the correct position and the girth is tight enough to prevent it slipping around or sliding back. If no one else is holding your horse, keep an arm through the reins while you adjust the girths and stirrup leathers and pull down the stirrup irons. Never leave him loose – even the most quiet horse can take fright and may take off, with disastrous consequences. As you prepare to mount, make sure that your horse is standing still and squarely, ready to take your weight. Also practice getting on and off from the other side as an exercise in versatility.

OBJECTIVE: To arrive in the saddle with the minimum of fuss, prepared for riding away. *Rating* ●●●

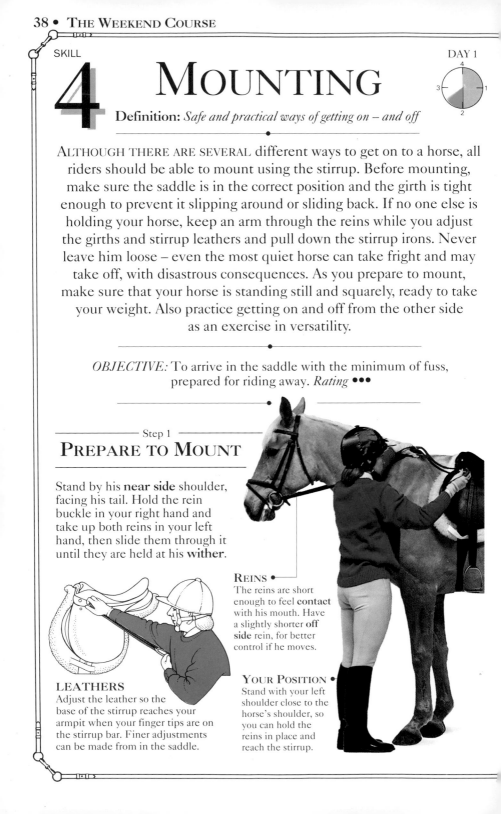

—— Step 1 ——
PREPARE TO MOUNT

Stand by his **near side** shoulder, facing his tail. Hold the rein buckle in your right hand and take up both reins in your left hand, then slide them through it until they are held at his **wither**.

REINS
The reins are short enough to feel **contact** with his mouth. Have a slightly shorter **off side** rein, for better control if he moves.

LEATHERS
Adjust the leather so the base of the stirrup reaches your armpit when your finger tips are on the stirrup bar. Finer adjustments can be made from in the saddle.

YOUR POSITION
Stand with your left shoulder close to the horse's shoulder, so you can hold the reins in place and reach the stirrup.

• **REIN**
Drop the buckle end of
the rein to his **off side**,
out of the way.

Step 2
FOOT IN THE STIRRUP

Turn the stirrup towards you, using
your right hand. Stand on your right
foot and put your left foot into the iron.
Keep control with the reins.

STIRRUPS
Bring the far side
of the stirrup
towards you so
the leather hangs
flat under your
leg when you are
in the saddle.

• **FOOT**
Put most of your foot in
the stirrup and press
down with your toe.

• **RIGHT LEG**
Keep your weight over
your right leg as you
raise the left one.

Step 3
SPRINGING UP

Grip the seat with the right
hand. Transfer your weight to
your left foot. Keep your left toe down
and, leaning towards the horse, spring
up and pivot around to face forwards.

LEFT HAND •
Keep a light
contact with his
mouth. You could
also grasp his mane.

LEFT KNEE •
Press your left knee
close to the saddle,
keeping your boot
clear of his side. Hop
round on your right
foot to face inwards.

RIGHT WAY
As you turn, the leather
hangs vertically and
away from his side.

WRONG WAY
Don't dig your toe
into the horse – it
may make him move.

SKILL

4

RIGHT LEG OVER & LANDING

As you spring up, raise your right leg over the cantle, and move your right hand forward. Once in the saddle, put your right foot into the right stirrup.

• RIGHT LEG
Avoid touching the horse's back.

BODY •
Move carefully and lightly so that your weight does not drag the saddle toward you.

MOUNTING NOTE
Using a **mounting block** requires less effort and is more comfortable for your horse as you are much less likely to pull his saddle round.

LANDING
Right: Lower yourself gently into the saddle, never land heavily. Feel for the right stirrup with your right foot turned inwards.

DISMOUNTING

Leaving the saddle

CORRECT
Remove your feet from the stirrups and take both reins in your left hand. Rest your right hand on the front of the saddle and lean forward, putting your weight over your hand. Lift your right leg clear of the horse's back and drop gently to the ground, landing upright beside his shoulder. Avoid kicking his fore leg as you go down. Absorb the impact of the drop by landing on your toes with your knees bent.

INCORRECT
Never dismount by throwing your leg over the horse's **withers**. If you do this you will have to drop the reins and lose all control. If he moves away you could fall off backwards onto your head.

ALTERNATIVE MOUNTING

*Other methods of mounting include using a **mounting block**, or having a "leg up".*
If you are particularly agile, try vaulting on

VAULTING ON

Only the most athletic riders are able to vault onto their horse. Like using a **mounting block**, vaulting does not drag the saddle round.

1. SPRINGING UP
With your left hand holding the reins at his **withers** and your right hand across the seat of the saddle, bend your knees and spring up.

2. INTO THE SADDLE
Using your arms as leverage, push yourself up high enough to be able to swing your right leg over the saddle and his back without brushing them.

FACING FORWARDS

Turn the left edge of the stirrup towards you, point your toe forwards, and make room for your right leg as it leaves the ground. If your horse moves, you can go with him.

HAVING A LEG UP

Face the saddle, reins in the left hand, right hand on the seat. Bend your left leg so an assistant can support it. The assistant raises your left leg as you spring up, lifting your right leg over the horse's back.

SKILL

DAY 1

5 IN THE SADDLE

Definition: *Adjusting your position before you move off*

BEFORE YOU CAN SIT and hold the reins correctly, your saddle must be secured in the right position and your stirrups adjusted to a practical length. Once settled in the saddle, a few simple exercises will improve your balance and make you feel secure. They will also help you to acquire an **independent seat**, which will allow you to be in harmony with your horse's movement at all paces.

OBJECTIVE: To sit safely and comfortably in the saddle, correctly balanced over the horse's center of gravity. *Rating* •••••

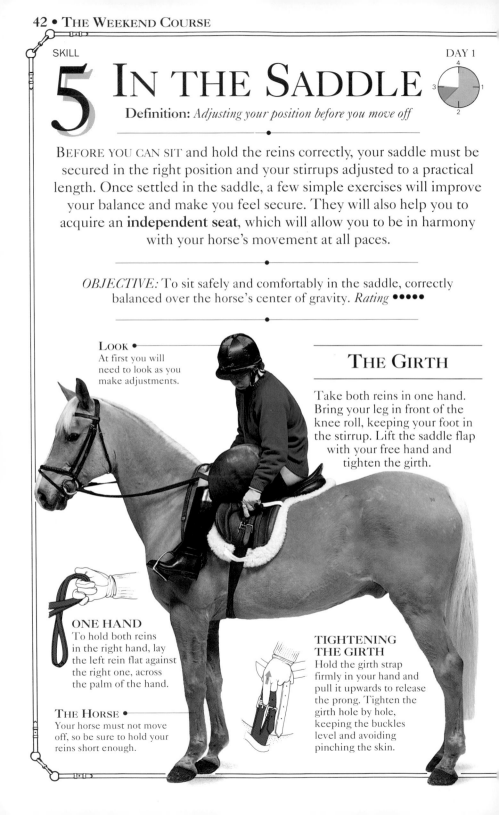

LOOK •
At first you will need to look as you make adjustments.

THE GIRTH

Take both reins in one hand. Bring your leg in front of the knee roll, keeping your foot in the stirrup. Lift the saddle flap with your free hand and tighten the girth.

ONE HAND
To hold both reins in the right hand, lay the left rein flat against the right one, across the palm of the hand.

THE HORSE •
Your horse must not move off, so be sure to hold your reins short enough.

TIGHTENING THE GIRTH
Hold the girth strap firmly in your hand and pull it upwards to release the prong. Tighten the girth hole by hole, keeping the buckles level and avoiding pinching the skin.

REINS •
Hold both your
reins in one hand.

THE STIRRUPS

As a guide, the stirrup leathers are a
suitable length if the base of the stirrup
reaches to your ankle joint when you
dangle your leg down. Practice
adjusting your stirrup lengths until you
can do it without having to
look at what you are doing.

• **LEG**
Keeping your foot in the
stirrup, draw back your leg
slightly to gain easier access
to the buckle.

SHORTENING THE LEATHERS
Pull the leather up to free
the prong. Guide it into the
right hole with your first
finger. Pull down on the
inside of the leather to
move the buckle to the top.

STIRRUP LENGTHS

GENERAL PURPOSE
A medium length leather is
most practical for learning.
It allows a balanced and
comfortable position.

JUMPING
Shorter leathers close the
angles at the hip, knee, and
ankle joints, for flexibility
and shock-absorption.

DRESSAGE
"Long legs", as used for
dressage, are most effective,
but are only possible if you
have a strong, deep seat.

TAKING UP THE REINS

You will need to adjust the reins as soon as you get on so that you establish **contact** *with your horse's mouth and prevent him from moving off*

Step 1

SHORTENING

It is important to shorten your reins quickly, yet smoothly and evenly. First, take the rein buckle in your left hand.

2. Take up the right rein in your right hand – hold it correctly (see opposite).

3. Grasp the left rein with your right thumb and forefinger, so that your left hand is freed.

4. Take the left rein in your left hand and hold it correctly at the required length.

5. Using the thumb and first finger of your left hand, take the free end of the right rein.

6. Draw the right rein through your right hand until it is the same length as the left rein.

7. Now the reins are of equal length, adjust your hands for even **contact** with his mouth.

HOLDING THE REINS

You must learn how to hold the reins correctly before you can use them. They should be equal in length, without twists, and should maintain a light, even **contact**. The arms should be relaxed – allowing your hands to act independently from the rest of the body, able to give and take at all times. Good communication with your horse depends on your sensitivity.

SINGLE REINS

From the bit, the rein passes between your little and third fingers, across your palm, to be held between your thumb and first finger. Keep your hands level, about 10cm (4in) apart, just above the **withers**.

DOUBLE REINS

Double reins may be held in several ways, but most often the snaffle, or bridoon, rein goes outside the **curb** rein with a finger separating the two. The two reins are then held together under the thumb.

Your thumb should face upwards. Hold the reins firmly without gripping tightly, keep your fingers closed yet gentle

The free end of the rein hangs between the rein and his neck. It must not go over the rein as this interferes with balance

FAULTY HAND POSITIONS

It is all too easy to develop faults – check your hands frequently until the correct position is second nature. Watch out for these common faults. With palms down, the tendons of the wrists and arms are twisted and stiff. The reverse – palms up, with the fingers turned up, and stiff, hollow wrists – makes the hands too tense. Open hands, with loose fingers, allow the reins to slip through and become too long. Curled or bent wrists lose their elasticity. Don't allow either hand to cross over his neck.

Palms down

Palms up

Open hands

Curled wrists

SKILL

5

THE RIDING POSITION

To communicate effectively with your horse while remaining secure,
you must develop and then establish a deep, strong, and well-balanced seat

CLASSICAL SEAT

Sit deep in the saddle, with your thighs and knees pressed down, close to the horse. Keep the balls of your feet on the stirrups, toes forwards and heels down. Let your arms hang naturally, and keep your joints supple.

REAR VIEW
Sit centrally, feet level, so that a vertical line can be drawn from the top of your head, through his tail to the ground.

• HEAD
Carry your head up and look forwards without tension in your neck.

• ARMS
A line is formed from your elbow, through the reins, to the bit.

SHOULDERS TO HEELS •
Hold your shoulders naturally and level, not rounded or stiff. They should form an imaginary vertical line from elbow to heel.

KNEE TO TOE •
Your lower leg slopes back slightly. Your knee and toe are roughly in line and the stirrup leather hangs vertically.

A FAULTY POSITION

It is important to be taught a good position from the beginning. However, it is better to find a balanced seat naturally than to force your body into it, causing tension and preventing good communication with your horse.

REAR VIEW

By sitting to the left this rider has lost his **balance**. To counteract this he has "collapsed" his right hip and leans to the right.

The green lines indicate the extent of the rider's position faults

THE REINS •
Tension in the arms and hands is communicated to the horse through taut reins.

BODY •
The body is tipped behind the vertical, and the rider looks stiff, as though he is trying too hard!

COMMON POSITION FAULTS

Chair seat

Here are some typical faults that affect the rider's **balance** and use of the **aids**. They include: the *chair seat*, sitting at the back of the saddle with legs forward; an exaggerated *forward seat*, tipping forward over the horse's shoulder with legs back; *elbows out* with tense, fixed arms; and *knees out*, which forces out the toes; a *hollow back*, with the rider stiffening his body; and *toes down*, a very common fault.

Knees and elbows out

Toes down

Hollow back

Forward seat

SKILL
5

EXERCISES AT THE HALT

*Exercises in the saddle, when stationary, will improve your balance
and security, and help you develop an **independent seat***

ARM SWINGS
Keeping your legs
still, stretch your
arms out and
swing them left
and right.

WITH STIRRUPS

At first you will feel safer keeping your
stirrups when doing exercises without
reins. It also enables you to retain a
good position. These exercises
will help you to overcome
stiffness and relax your joints,
tendons, and muscles.

**STANDING
IN THE STIRRUPS**
Stand in the stirrups, balanced
on the balls of your feet, with
your heels taking most of your
weight. Then raise your arms
to shoulder level. The stirrup
leathers must hang straight.

• **REINS**
The reins are
knotted, ready to
hold if he moves.
Grab a **neckstrap**
or his mane if you
lose your balance.

• **LEGS**
Keeping your heels
directly below your
hips, straighten
your knees and
stretch your thighs.

• **THE HORSE**
Only a reliable horse,
which will stand still,
should be used for these
exercises. An assistant
should be ready to hold
him if necessary.

WITHOUT STIRRUPS

When you are confident enough to do exercises without stirrups, you will benefit even more. It will strengthen your seat and increase your flexibility and co-ordination. They can be quite strenuous so build them up gradually.

LEGS
Lower your legs carefully.

RAISING ARMS AND LEGS
Stretch up from your waist and lift your legs outwards, pressing down in the saddle.

LEANING BACKWARDS
Lean back, until you are resting on his rump, then sit up again. Your legs should stay in place – not easy!

POLL TOUCH
Stretch an arm forward to touch the poll. Then sit up and change arms. Keep your lower legs in the correct position.

TOE TOUCH
Left: Touch your left toe with your right hand, then your right toe with your left hand.

LEGS
Keep your legs in position.

ARM ROTATION
Right: Sit squarely, and swing or rotate one arm by your side, keeping it straight and reaching up high. Change arms.

SKILL

6 FIRST STEPS

DAY 1

Definition: *Moving off, turning, and stopping using simple aids*

HAVING WORKED HARD to obtain a correct and secure position, you can now learn to apply basic **aids** for control. These become more complicated as you progress, but to begin with you only need to know how to move forward, make simple turns, and stop. A well-trained horse should respond to fairly light aids, teaching you to be tactful and accurate. To make a clean **transition** (change of pace), you must learn to co-ordinate the use of your legs, hands, and seat, with the necessary degree of intensity, at the right time, and in the right place.

OBJECTIVE: To give effective **aids** and to maintain position when moving from halt to walk, walk to halt, and when turning at the walk. *Rating* ●●●●

— THE AIDS —

"Aids" are the signals for communicating with your horse. Natural aids are given by your legs, hands, seat, and voice. Artificial aids are extras like whips and spurs. To apply aids efficiently you must be able to maintain the correct position, without being too tense or too slack. Always apply aids gently at first. Repeat them with more strength, if necessary, but always return to light aids to maintain sensitivity.

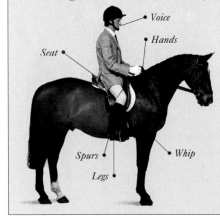

Voice

Hands

Seat

Spurs

Whip

Legs

LEGS
Your legs tell your horse to go faster, to keep him straight or turn him. Apply the lower part of your legs against his sides, just behind the girth, to go forward. Use them further back to guide his quarters. When not giving an aid, keep them still.

HANDS (REINS)
Hands help control and guide your horse. Every rein aid is followed by yielding your hands. "Good" hands are sensitive and light; they maintain a steady **contact**, following his movement. Don't use your hands to punish your horse.

SEAT (WEIGHT)
As your seat becomes established, it will play a greater part in influencing your horse. You can change his balance by slight body movements, and you can use your seat muscles, with leg aids, to produce energy, to prepare for **transitions**, and to warn him of any following instructions.

VOICE
The voice is effective if used sparingly, to soothe, praise, or scold your horse.

HALT TO WALK

*Prepare for moving off by keeping your horse attentive, and by sitting correctly, so you can give the **aids** with minimum movement or effort*

HALT
Your horse should be standing squarely, so that he can push forwards with his hind legs.

TRANSITION
Brace your back, squeeze with your legs, and keep a light, even **contact** with your horse's mouth.

WALK
Feel the four-time beat of the walk (see Gaits pp.12-13). Let your hands follow the motion of his head.

TRANSITION

Aim for an even, regular walk which is calm, yet active and purposeful. The horse should go straight. Learn to judge how much pressure you should apply for the required result.

SEAT
Sit deep, bracing your spine, to create forward movement and energy. When he is moving, relax your spine and seat muscles.

HANDS
Maintain a sensitive **contact** with the reins. Guide him and regulate his energy.

LEGS
Apply your legs firmly, just behind the girth. A sensitive horse only needs a squeeze, but others need stronger legs.

SKILL

6

TURNING

When riding a turn, your legs, body, and hands have separate roles.
*Your horse should **bend** in the direction he is going*

TURNING ON A CIRCLE

When making a turn or circle, the horse's
hind feet must follow directly in the track
of his fore feet, and his frame follows the arc
of the circle. Your legs guide and control his
hindquarters; your reins direct his **forehand**.

INCORRECT TURNS

Some don'ts when turning:
- Don't go so far into a corner that his hind legs can't follow.
- Don't let him fall in on his shoulder, so bending the wrong way. If he does, correct it with your inside leg, not your hands.
- Don't pull your horse's head around, bending his neck too much and losing control of his shoulders and hindquarters.

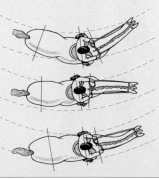

SHOULDER OUT
The inside rein is too short,
causing too much bend and
throwing his shoulder out.

SHOULDER IN
The horse carries his head
to the outside and falls
in on his shoulder.

HAND OUT
Pulling the horse around
with the inside rein will
throw him off balance.

QUARTERS OUT
The horse does not bend
properly or take his weight
over his inside hind leg.

AIDS TO TURNING

On a turn, your legs and body have more influence than your hands, which should be used as little as possible. Aim to keep up the same rhythm throughout the turn, judging the amount of **impulsion** or **bend** needed, and adjusting the **aids** accordingly.

HEAD •
Turn your head to look directly between your horse's ears.

• BODY
Sit squarely in the saddle. Don't slide out or lean in.

INSIDE HAND •
The inside rein guides him into the bend but is held lightly, so that it is not blocking his inside shoulder.

INSIDE LEG •
The inside leg stays close to the girth, maintaining **impulsion** and controlling the amount of **bend**.

Inside leg

SHOULDERS •
Keep your shoulders parallel with your horse's shoulders.

• OUTSIDE HAND
Keep a firm **contact** on the outside rein, to control the pace and the bend, and to keep the outside shoulder in line with the bend.

• HIPS
Your hips turn in the direction of the bend, parallel with your horse's hips.

• OUTSIDE LEG
The outside leg controls his quarters. Move it back slightly to stop them moving out or swinging.

Outside leg

WALK TO HALT

*To bring him into a straight, squarely-balanced halt, the horse must
be prepared, and held with leg, weight, and rein **aids** (see Aids p.50)*

WALK
Sit deep, using your legs to
make sure his hind legs are
well underneath, and gently
warn him with the reins.

TRANSITION
Straighten your back, bracing
your seat muscles. Press your
lower legs in and increase
your feel on the reins.

HALT
Continue with slight aids to
go forward and ease your
reins without losing **contact**.
The halt should be square.

TRANSITION

To make a smooth transition to
halt, without resistance, always
prepare your horse so that he
brings his hind legs under him,
distributing his weight evenly
over hind and fore legs.

• POSITION
Prepare him by straightening
your back and pressing down
into the saddle, tightening
your seat and thigh muscles.

• HANDS
Feel his mouth,
using a taking and
yielding action.
Increase the feel
if necessary, but
never pull on the
reins. Use both
hands equally.

LEGS •
Apply your legs, just
behind the girth, to
control his quarters.

REIN BACK

The rein back is when the horse steps back with alternate diagonal pairs of legs. Usually performed from a **square halt**, it is a test of obedience, suppleness, and straightness. It also tests your use of the correct **aids**. His steps should be regular, straight, and of good length, and he must not resist by raising his head, hollowing his back, showing reluctance, deviating to one side, or rushing. He should maintain a correct outline.

Riding forward   *Moving back*   *Square halt*

POSITION •
Horse and rider are well positioned to go forwards or backwards.

• CONTACT
Keep a definite contact with legs and hands.

SQUARE HALT
A good halt is one that is balanced squarely over all four legs. Your horse is straight and remains still, but he is attentive to your **aids**, which are maintained. He is ready to move forwards again, at any given pace, or perhaps to go backwards.

• THE HORSE
As he backs, keep him straight with your legs and hands.

MOVING BACK
From a good **square halt**, press down with your seat and thighs and close your legs, asking for a forward movement. At the moment that he wants to step forward, close your hands. When he feels slight resistance, he will release his **impulsion** backwards. Sit up straight to encourage him and prevent him resisting. Ride him forwards after a few steps.

• LEGS
He lifts his near hind and off fore legs together to step back.

SKILL

7 TROTTING

DAY 2

Definition: *Learning the sitting and rising trot*

ONCE YOU FEEL CONFIDENT at the walk you may progress to learning to trot. This swinging gait is bouncy and may unbalance you at first, mainly because you are likely to tense your body against it, gripping tightly to stay in the saddle. However, the less you try, the easier it becomes. Use a **neckstrap**, or grab some mane, or the pommel, to steady yourself without jerking on the reins. At first, try sitting to the trot. Relax, don't cling on, and allow your lower back to absorb the motion. Eventually you will stay in position using balance, not grip. **Posting**, when you can do it, is less tiring for you and your horse.

OBJECTIVE: To sit and rise to the trot, without losing **balance** or position, and to control your horse at the trot and in **transitions**. *Rating* •••••

TROTTING PRACTICE

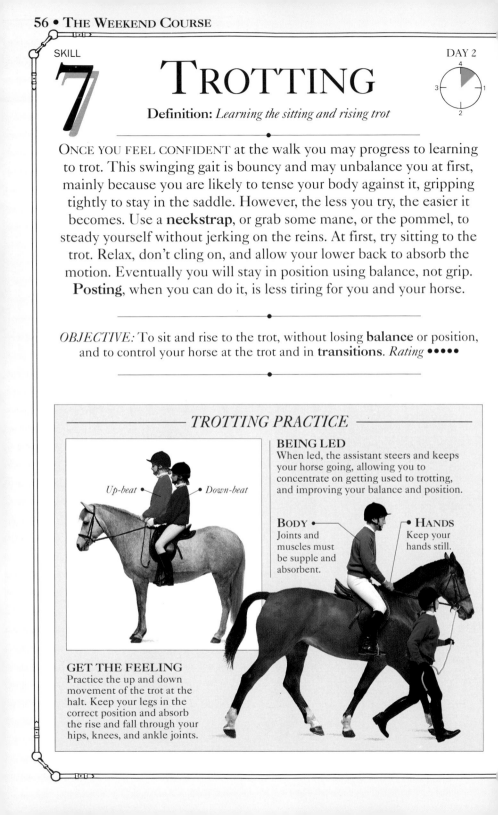

Up-beat • • *Down-beat*

BEING LED
When led, the assistant steers and keeps your horse going, allowing you to concentrate on getting used to trotting, and improving your balance and position.

BODY •
Joints and muscles must be supple and absorbent.

• **HANDS**
Keep your hands still.

GET THE FEELING
Practice the up and down movement of the trot at the halt. Keep your legs in the correct position and absorb the rise and fall through your hips, knees, and ankle joints.

WALK TO TROT

*To trot, use the same **aids** as for walking from the halt, only a little stronger, and remain sitting until you feel a regular trot rhythm*

WALK
Make sure the walk is active and your hands are in light **contact** with his mouth.

TRANSITION
Increase his attention by using stronger **aids**, pressing him with your seat and legs.

SITTING
For effective **aids** and balance, remain seated during the first strides.

POSTING
Start to rise when you feel the trot rhythm. Go with him, leaning slightly forward.

TRANSITION

Prepare to trot from an active walk by bracing your back, pressing down with your seat muscles, and feeling a definite **contact** via the reins. Squeeze with both legs, as strongly as necessary (kick, if he doesn't respond), encouraging him into a trot with allowing hands.

• HEAD
Keep your head up and try not to tense your neck. If you do, it will affect the suppleness of your spine.

• BODY
Square your shoulders, staying upright over his center of balance. Sit as deep in the saddle as possible and keep your hands still.

• LEGS
Squeeze with both legs, then release. Keep them still and firmly in place once he has responded.

SKILL

7

POSITION
Rise as his off fore
leg touches down.

RISING TROT

To **post** at the trot, you move up
and down from your knees, with
elastic ankle and hip joints. Your
legs stay still, with unvarying
contact. Don't let your shoulders
get ahead of your knees or toes.
Keep your hands steady. Trotting
on the right diagonal is shown
here; to change the diagonal, sit
for an extra "bump".

POSITION
Sit as his off fore
leg touches down.

UP-BEAT
As one diagonal pair of legs leaves
the ground, allow yourself to be
pushed up. Lean forward slightly
to avoid getting left behind on the
down-beat. How high you rise
depends on your horse's action.

DOWN-BEAT
As the same pair of legs returns
to the ground, so you return
lightly to the saddle. It may
help to count aloud, "up-down-
up-down" until you have
mastered **posting**.

THE SITTING TROT

BODY
Avoid bumping
about, by letting
your body move
with the rhythm.

The sitting trot will become comfortable
for you and your horse once you can absorb
the bouncy movement without gripping or
tensing your body against it. At first, it will
help if you trot slowly on a calm horse with
even paces, and preferably on the lunge
(see Skill 8 p.60). Every part of you needs
to be relaxed and act as a shock-absorber,
so that you can retain a deep seat and give
clear, controlled **aids** to influence his pace,
rhythm, balance, and direction. Unlike for
posting, you remain completely upright at
sitting trot, in the same position as for
walk. Exercises will loosen you up, and
when you feel both comfortable and safe
while sitting correctly, you can strengthen
your position by trotting without stirrups.

TROT TO WALK

*To make a smooth **transition** from the rising trot to walk, prepare your horse by sitting in the saddle and keeping him balanced*

TROT
Maintain a normal, active trot, but warn your horse of what is to come by bracing your back and seat muscles.

TRANSITION
Sit for the transition, driving your horse forward with your seat and legs into hands that hold him, so slowing him.

WALK
When he walks, immediately yield with your hands, on supple arms, to allow him freedom to walk on actively.

TRANSITION

To make a smooth **transition** without resistance from his mouth or neck, sit in the saddle so that you keep close contact with your horse, and give clear **aids**. Never use your hands alone, but co-ordinate them with seat and legs so he doesn't lose momentum or balance.

• HEAD
Look forward, keeping your head up. Don't tense your neck.

• BODY
Use your back and seat muscles to drive him forward into even rein contact. How much pressure you need depends on the response that you get.

• HANDS
Your hands close momentarily to discourage forward movement, but are ready to yield again. Repeat more strongly, if you have to, but never pull him back.

LEGS •
Press down with your thighs, and squeeze him with your lower leg to ride him forward into the rein **contact** for a balanced **transition**.

SKILL

8

LESSONS ON THE LUNGE

DAY 2

Definition: *Improving your balance, security, and co-ordination in the saddle*

RIDING ON A LUNGE helps to establish an **independent seat**. Once this is achieved, your progress should be rapid. A calm and obedient horse, which keeps an even, steady rhythm at walk and trot, is vital for lungeing as it allows the instructor to concentrate on you. Exercises at the walk will teach you how to use different parts of your body separately. They improve your seat and **balance**, and give you the confidence to progress to trotting on the lunge without the use of reins – when security and balance become even more important.

OBJECTIVE: To acquire a safe, secure, and **balanced** position enabling effective use of the **aids**. *Rating* •••••

LUNGEING EQUIPMENT

Lungeing equipment consists of the lunge rein, a cavesson, side reins, and boots or bandages for protection. A lungeing whip is also necessary.

THE INSTRUCTOR
The instructor wears gloves for protection. She controls the horse with the lunge rein and whip. The horse moves in a circle around her.

• LUNGE REIN
The rein is about 10m (33ft) long.

CAVESSON •
The cavesson can be used alone, or fitted over a bridle, as here. It must fit so that it does not slip or rub when the lunge rein pulls on the ring attachments.

SIDE REINS •
The side reins, which help balance and control the horse, are attached to the girth straps.

WALKING ON THE LUNGE

*Exercises at the walk teach you to use the different parts of your
body separately and will help you to gain confidence*

A MORE SECURE SEAT

The lower you sit in the saddle,
the stronger your position.
Keep your feet in the stirrups
until you feel safe and can
stay upright over the
center of balance.

SEAT EXERCISE

Remove or cross your
stirrups. Press your knees
and ankles down to stretch
your legs straight. Lift
them away from the
saddle. As you relax
them back again,
stretch them down
and sit tall.

BETTER BALANCE

Good **balance** is the basis of successful
riding. Exercises on the lunge help you
maintain your position without
gripping with legs and knees.
Between exercises, resume the
upright position, with a straight
back and square shoulders.

Body twist

Head rotation

Arm circles

EXERCISES FOR BALANCE

Activate your muscles, and increase suppleness,
by putting hands on your hips and twisting your
body from the waist. Rotating your head, one
way, then the other, will loosen your neck and
help to relax your shoulders. Hold your arms
out, then circle them, alternately or both
together. This improves your co-ordination.

8 TROTTING ON THE LUNGE

*On the lunge, the instructor controls your horse and maintains the rhythm and pace, while you learn to **balance** without using your hands*

SITTING TROT

The sitting trot is done at a steady pace. It may be tiring at first and you should have frequent breaks. Gradually, you will learn to relax and absorb the motion, instead of bumping up and down.

POSITION
Start by holding onto the pommel, then practice keeping your hands still, just above your horse's **withers**. Your posture is the same as it is for the walk – upright but not stiff, with a constant leg position.

• NECKSTRAP
If you lose your balance or feel insecure, hold onto the **neckstrap**.

TROTTING EXERCISES

• BACK STRAIGHT
Fold your arms behind your back to straighten your spine and square your shoulders.

When you can keep your balance at a trot, improve and strengthen your riding position with some of these exercises. They will also help you to loosen up and feel more confident.

LOOSENING UP
Right: Tense shoulders restrict the reflexes and action of your arm, including elbows, wrists, and fingers. Shrugging or circling your shoulders will loosen the shoulder blades. Do the movements separately, then practice this exercise to draw the shoulders back.

BETTER LUNGEING

Trotting on the lunge is the most effective way to acquire the firm, deep, balanced seat that is necessary for good riding. However, with the wrong approach it can turn into a painful and even frightening experience. For safe, successful, and comfortable lungeing it is essential to have a good instructor and a reliable horse.

THE INSTRUCTOR
As you are not holding the reins, your instructor has control, so you need to feel confident that she knows what she is doing. A good instructor will keep the horse at a steady pace. She will relax you a little and then put you through a series of exercises to work on your individual weaknesses and to improve your suppleness and co-ordination.

THE HORSE
It is essential to lunge with a mature, placid, obedient horse that does not get upset by his rider's tenseness, sudden loss of **balance**, or any unexpected actions that may occur. He must be able to maintain a smooth, regular, steady trot.

TROTTING WITHOUT STIRRUPS
Trotting without stirrups should not be attempted until you feel secure and well-balanced with stirrups. You must feel absolutely confident that your instructor has control and that your horse is not going to do anything that will unbalance you. A **neckstrap** is useful for grabbing if you feel unsafe. Concentrate on stretching your legs down, straight and long. Relax your upper body to absorb the two-time trot motion.

IMPROVING BALANCE
Below left: Exercises like these help improve your **balance** and straighten your spine. If you maintain the correct leg position it is easier to remain upright.

• ARMS UP
Raise your arms above your head, stretching up from the waist.

REMOVING TENSION
Below right: Simple exercises help overcome problems caused by tension or stiffness. By balancing over your feet, you develop a secure seat without using your hands and increase your confidence.

• HANDS ON HIPS
Rest your hands on your hips and relax your shoulders and elbows.

SKILL

9 GROUP RIDING

DAY 2

Definition: *Learning how to control your horse in a group lesson*

RIDING IN COMPANY WILL improve your understanding of how a horse behaves with other horses. Ideally, a group lesson is held in an enclosed arena, with corners, straight sides, and guiding markers. The lesson may begin with an inspection of riders and tack, some general advice, and an assessment of the overall standard. You may do exercises at walk and trot, and work without stirrups. You will learn to ride **transitions**, turns, and school figures (see pp.66-67), together and individually, with periods of rest for discussion and to watch others.

OBJECTIVE: To improve your use of the **aids**, to sharpen your reactions and awareness, and to develop a sense of rhythm and timing. *Rating* ••••

CHANGING PACE

The instructor will always warn you before an increase or decrease in pace, so that you can prepare your horse.

• **PACE SETTER**
The leader maintains an even pace, which is not too fast or too slow. This enables the others to keep up without being impeded.

KEEP RIDING
It is easier just to allow your horse to follow the one in front, but you will not learn anything. You must use the **aids**, as you would when riding alone, to make him go into the corners, and turn, and change speed when you ask him to.

PASSING SIDE BY SIDE

Leave about 1.5m (5ft) between horses when you are passing in opposite directions, even more when overtaking. If too close, your horse may **shy**, rush, or threaten to kick, or he may try to stop and follow his friend, and will need to be ridden strongly.

• THINK AHEAD
Stay alert, plan ahead, and anticipate the actions of others.

RIDE STRAIGHT •
Hold your horse's attention and keep him straight **between hand and leg** as you pass.

GETTING TOO CLOSE
If your horse's normal pace and rhythm are obstructed by others, ask if you may circle away, or take the lead. Always leave enough space between horses – at least half a horse's length – so you can take evasive action to avoid getting kicked or having a collision.

• KEEPING UP
Don't drop behind. It can disrupt a lesson if you do not keep up. Be determined; some horses become lazy, and need strong riding.

• THE INSTRUCTOR
The instructor stands where she can see the whole group. She gives clear directions as to who should do what; and where; and when they should do it.

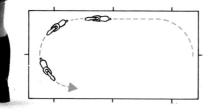

CHANGING THE LEADER
This exercise begins with the ride walking in single file. The leader trots on and rejoins at the back of the ride. He starts at a sitting trot, progresses to **posting**, then sits to give the **aids** for the walk. Each new leader does the same.

SKILL

9

CHANGING DIRECTION

To change direction, or **change the rein**, give definite **aids** which your horse should obey immediately. Practice at a walk, turning from the right rein (clockwise) to the left rein (counter-clockwise) smoothly and accurately, changing the bend. When trotting, plan well ahead to maintain **balance** and rhythm on the turn.

— *SCHOOL FIGURES* —

A standard arena of 40 x 20m (130 x 66ft) with markers, is ideal for school exercises, most of which are based on circles.

The exercises here are: 1. Circles of 20m (66ft) and 10m (33ft) in diameter; 2. **Changing the rein**, by crossing the arena diagonally at the quarter markers, or in a figure of eight; 3. Crossing the center, either at the half markers (B to E), or down the center line (A to C), which needs preparation as it involves tight turns; 4. Serpentine loops, or half circles of 15m (50ft) and 10m (33ft); 5. A series of 3-5m (10-16ft) loops, along the edge of the arena, using cones as markers.

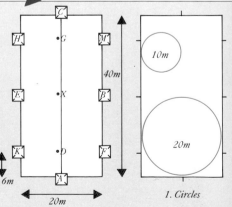

1. Circles

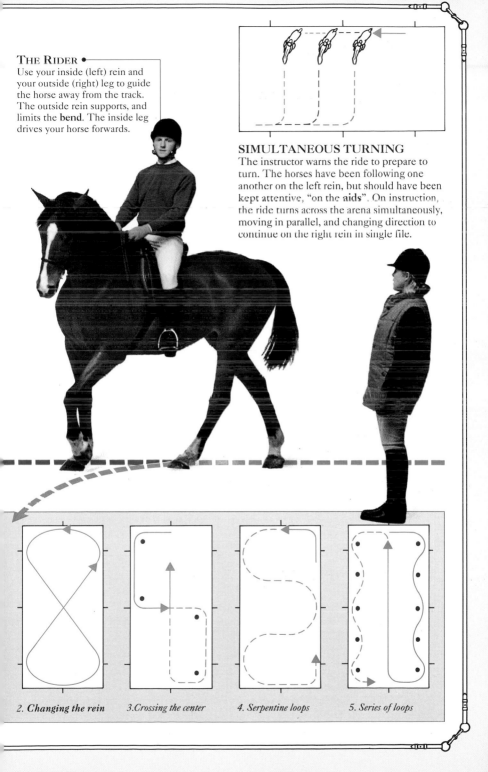

THE RIDER •
Use your inside (left) rein and
your outside (right) leg to guide
the horse away from the track.
The outside rein supports, and
limits the **bend**. The inside leg
drives your horse forwards.

SIMULTANEOUS TURNING
The instructor warns the ride to prepare to
turn. The horses have been following one
another on the left rein, but should have been
kept attentive, "on the **aids**". On instruction,
the ride turns across the arena simultaneously,
moving in parallel, and changing direction to
continue on the right rein in single file.

2. Changing the rein   *3.Crossing the center*   *4. Serpentine loops*   *5. Series of loops*

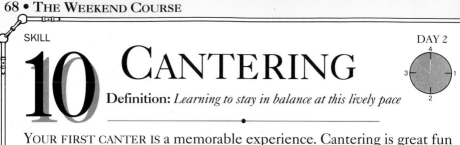

10 CANTERING

Definition: *Learning to stay in balance at this lively pace*

YOUR FIRST CANTER IS a memorable experience. Cantering is great fun – when it is well controlled. At first, you may be tense and bounce about, as the pace seems so fast, but when you learn to move in harmony with the slightly rocking motion, it is very comfortable. The canter is a bounding pace, with each stride followed by a period of **suspension**. When the near fore leg strikes the ground ahead of the off fore, it is a canter on the left **lead**, and when the off fore leg leads it is a canter on the right lead. On a straight line, either leg may lead, but on a turn or circle, the inside pair (both fore and hind legs) must be leading for the horse to keep his balance.

OBJECTIVE: To **strike-off** into canter on the correct **lead**, to control the pace, and to return smoothly from canter to trot. *Rating* ●●●●

CANTERING FAULTS

Out of control

Spoiling the balance

Most faults in the **transition** to canter occur because the horse is not prepared for changing pace. **Striking-off** on the wrong leg is caused by an unbalanced trot, bending to the outside, or using incorrect **aids.** When the reins are too long and have no contact on his mouth, the **transition** is uncontrolled. The horse may trot faster and faster (above left), eventually falling into a flat, unbalanced canter. The rider is balancing on her hands instead of over her feet, and the horse has too much weight on his **forehand.** Leaning over the horse's shoulder to see what leg is **leading** (above right), is also unbalancing. Other faults include: gripping with legs, which prevents you from giving efficient aids; hanging on with the hands; swinging legs; and rocking the body back and forth. All are caused by a poor position or tension.

TROT TO CANTER

*Control the **impulsion**, ready to release it into a canter. It is easier to ask for a*
*__transition__ on a corner or bend as it helps you to **strike-off** on the correct leg*

TROT
To prepare for canter to the right, sit down and tighten your seat muscles. Hold him together with legs and hands.

TRANSITION
Flex him slightly to the right, and use your inside (right) leg close to the girth, placing your outside leg further back.

CANTER
Ease your rein, to give his right shoulder freedom, then maintain light **contact**. Keep him going with your legs.

TRANSITION

A good canter depends on the quality of the trot before the **transition**. When applying your seat and legs, don't let him quicken or lengthen his stride. Sit straight and upright – try not to lean forward in anticipation.

• **HANDS**
Your inside hand asks for flexion. Your outside hand controls **bend** and **impulsion**.

LEGS •
Your inside leg creates energy, bringing his hind leg underneath him; your outside leg, behind the girth, stops his quarters swinging out.

SKILL

10 THE CANTER

Sit up straight, as for the walk, and let your hips go with your horse's movement so that your seat remains in the saddle. Hold a **neckstrap** or the pommel with one hand, until you feel safe.

• **BODY**
Try not to tense up. Relax your shoulders and hips to absorb the motion. Keep your arms elastic to allow him a steady head-carriage.

LEGS •
Maintain the energy by keeping your legs firmly in place. When turning, the outside leg may move back to guide the quarters. A stronger leg **aid** is sometimes needed to keep him going.

• **THE HORSE**
Keep him balanced, with his strides short and bouncy, otherwise he may break into a trot.

GETTING IT RIGHT

THE CORRECT LEG
The horse is **flexed** correctly to the left, and **leads** with his near fore and near hind legs for canter on the left. His inside hind takes most weight, keeping him balanced. If you are on the "wrong" leg (outside legs leading) or "disunited" (leading hind leg on the opposite side to leading fore leg), return to trot and prepare him again.

MAKING IT EASIER
The ideal place for the **transition** is the corner of the arena, because then the horse knows that he needs good balance on the correct leg to be able to turn. If this fails, ride him in a small circle in the corner and give the canter **aid** just before he returns to the track. With his inside hind leg well under him, he can push off it into a canter.

CANTER TO TROT

*The pace decreases when the **impulsion** that is generated by the horse's hindquarters
and maintained by the rider's seat and legs, meets hands that cease to yield*

CANTER
Brace your seat and legs, and hold a little more with your hands, to shorten his stride and lighten his **forehand**.

TRANSITION
Straighten your back and press down with your seat as you close your hands. His response decides the strength of the **aid**.

TROT
As he goes into trot, sit down in the saddle, yield with your hands, and resume a light contact with legs and hands.

TRANSITION

To make a smooth downward **transition**, your horse must not lose momentum or **balance**. If necessary, correct the canter first, warn him, then apply the **aid**.

• BODY
Sit deep in the saddle, but not too heavily. Prepare to adapt from the rocking canter to a sitting trot, absorbing the **transition**, which should be smooth and fluent.

• HANDS
Don't fix your hands, or pull. This will cause a loss of rhythm and, possibly, resistance.

LEGS •
Legs, seat, and hands must act together, to bring his hind legs under him enough to lighten his **forehand**. To trot, hold him with your legs, then lessen their pressure.

AFTER THE WEEKEND

Gaining more experience while developing basic techniques

YOU WILL PROBABLY NEED A REST after the intensive weekend course, to allow your aching body to recover! This time would be well spent on planning your future progress. Everything you have begun to learn during the weekend will need continual practice until it becomes habitual, and feels natural and comfortable. If possible it is best to continue in familiar surroundings, at the same riding school – especially if you got on well with the instructor and liked your horse. As you become more secure and in control, you will be able to enjoy riding out (hacking), away from the confines of the school. Each new experience, such as riding around fields, along paths, up and down hills, and over varying terrain, will test your skill. Eventually you must also learn to ride safely on roads, with an instructor, and in larger groups, and to cope with the unexpected when you meet pedestrians, livestock, noisy motorcycles, or other hazards.

More skills to learn

When you feel confident and can control your horse in difficult situations, you may want to learn to gallop and jump. Again your progress and enjoyment will depend on good instruction and the right horse. Joining your local riding club will introduce you to fellow riders, and may lead to activities such as trekking across country, riding holidays, or even competitive riding. You can also learn much from watching and listening to expert riders.

RIDING OUT

Hacking out in the countryside, and on roads and tracks

CONCENTRATED LEARNING becomes worthwhile when you progress to riding out, away from the school. Once you can control your mount in and around the training areas at all paces, keep your balance under normal circumstances, and have learned good horse sense, you are ready to test your skill. Practice in a field at first – horses tend to behave differently in a less confined situation, and to begin with you may find it more difficult to keep your position or control him. Do not abandon all you have learned, or become heavy-handed or casual! New experiences might include riding on variable surfaces, from hard roads to rough, overgrown, or muddy paths, through gateways, in woods, and up and down hills. You will need to ride competently to anticipate, and if possible avoid, hazards or problems ahead.

IN THE COUNTRY

Until you are familiar with riding in the country, try to ride with an experienced and reliable companion.

Follow these basic guidelines for a safe and pleasant ride.
• Plan your ride beforehand, deciding on your route and finding suitable stretches of ground where you may canter safely.
• Let someone at the stable know your route and when you expect to return.
• Be considerate to anyone riding behind or ahead of you – keep a steady pace and never overtake without warning.

• Be aware of your surroundings and always look ahead for possible hazards – avoid holes, litter, and boggy or slippery ground. If in doubt, walk.
• Beware of disturbing livestock and slow down to pass pedestrians and riders.
• Never ride on private land without first getting the owner's permission. Don't ride over crops, and always keep to the edge of fields, especially when the ground is wet.
• Always close any gates that you open on your ride (see below for how to open gates), even if the field looks empty.

1. Opening a gate will test your ability to give the right **aids**. Take the reins in one hand, lean down and unlatch and open the gate.

2. Keep hold of the gate as you guide your horse around it, using your legs firmly but carefully, so that he does not rush or back away.

3. Close the gate by turning on the **forehand** or making a small circle. Transfer the reins into your other hand, stand still, and fasten it.

A COUNTRY HACK

For your first hack you need to be riding a
reliable horse so that you can relax and enjoy
the experience. The accompanying horse
should also be well behaved so that the
instructor can concentrate on you.

THE RIDER
Look up and
ahead, and try to
relax your horse
will sense if you
are tense.

LEAD REIN
The instructor rides
with both reins in one
hand and leads with
the other.

LOW BRANCH
Duck under low
branches to avoid
being swept off !

GOING UPHILL
Lean forward when you are
riding uphill, allowing your
horse to use his hindquarters.
Let him stretch out his neck
as well. Don't get left behind!

THROUGH WATER
When going through water,
make sure the footing below
the water is firm and keep
your horse moving. Always
walk, unless it is very shallow.

GOING DOWNHILL
Keep to a walk, especially
if the hill is steep, and lean
forward a little. Don't allow
your legs to go back and
don't grip with your ankles.

ROAD RIDING

As a beginner, you should try to avoid riding on roads. However, if it is necessary, always ride a horse that is completely "traffic proof" and make sure you are thoroughly familiar with road regulations

TURNING

When you want to change direction, extend the appropriate arm for long enough to signal your intentions clearly. Never assume that a driver will stop and wait for you – some are very impatient. Plan ahead, judging when to move and when to wait.

LEFT TURN
When turning left, if the road is wide enough, move over to the center, after checking behind you. When it is clear, move across.

CHECK BEHIND
Look behind you frequently, especially when you are planning to turn. Always let drivers know in good time which way you are turning.

RIGHT TURN
Before turning right, give the signal by stretching out your right arm fully, so that it can be seen both from in front and behind.

— ROAD SAFETY —

Riding on roads can be dangerous, but these guidelines will help you keep out of trouble. Stay alert, and don't ride on a loose rein. Wear bright clothes if possible. Walk or trot slowly on the same side as the traffic, going with it. Use a grass verge if there is one, but watch out for litter. On narrow roads, ride single file. In a group, the rear rider waves on traffic, and the leader gives warning before changing pace or direction. Before passing hazards, such as road drills, make sure the road is clear. If you must ride on roads at night or in fog, wear **stirrup lights** and a fluorescent jacket.

ROAD ETIQUETTE

It is important to thank motorists when they are helpful. Thank them even if they barely slow down, otherwise next time they may go even faster! A large group should divide to let cars pass.

AVOIDING VEHICLES
Where possible get off the road. Here, the instructor is closest to the traffic, and the pupil is in a gateway.

NOD OR SMILE
Thank drivers with a nod or smile if you are not confident enough to remove a hand from the reins to salute them.

WARNING SIGNS

If you want to warn a driver to slow down or stop, look directly at him, making sure that he has seen you.

SLOW DOWN
Left: Extend your outside arm and wave it up and down to tell drivers you are about to slow down or halt. If a car is going too fast, signal to it to slow, then thank the driver.

STOP
Right: Hold up your hand, and look straight at the driver so he knows that you are signaling to him. Wait until the road is clear, then cross. Always keep close together if you are in a group.

JUMPING

Clearing obstacles – the approach, take-off, flight, and landing

GOOD **BALANCE** AND SECURITY are the keys to confident and successful jumping. The normal riding position is altered for jumping. This allows you to adjust to the four stages of the jump. A faulty position will upset your horse's balance, making jumping difficult and uncomfortable. Warm up by walking or trotting over poles on the ground, then practice cantering up and down hills in the jumping position before tackling single obstacles at trot and canter. You may then progress to grids, and riding a course of jumps.

JUMPING SEAT

Jumping requires a balanced, **forward seat**. Shorten the stirrup leathers (see p.43), and practice the position at a standstill. Then sustain it at a walk, at a trot, on turns, and over undulating terrain.

POSITION
Bend forward from your hips. Don't tip your shoulders ahead of your knees. Keep your head up – it is heavy and can upset your balance.

HANDS
Move your hands up the reins so that, with the arms and reins, they form a flowing line from elbow to bit. Keep the arms supple, allowing the horse to use his head and neck during flight.

LEGS
Keep your lower legs in place, close to the horse, with your toes up and ankles supple. Shorter stirrup lengths close the angles at your joints, providing greater shock-absorption.

PLACING POLES

RANDOM POLES

Place poles at random on an even surface. Practice walking over them at different angles. Then trot, using the jumping position, and practice keeping a rhythm. Try to judge distances between poles.

PARALLEL POLES

When poles are arranged parallel to each other they are usually positioned equal distances apart (about 1m (3ft) is ideal) so that the horse's feet land mid-way between each pole, when he is trotting.

TROTTING POLES

Line up 3-5 poles, spaced for trotting (see above). Walk over them first, then trot. The rhythm of the trot should not alter, and your position does not change, although your hands should allow his neck to lower and stretch a little.

• POSITION
Use the rising or sitting trot, but sit lightly, taking most weight in the stirrups so your horse can use his back freely. Practice inclining forward in the jumping position. Keep your head up, looking ahead. All joints must be supple.

• THE HORSE
The horse bends his knees and hocks to avoid touching the poles. He should lower his head and neck and swing his back, staying calm and relaxed.

• LEGS
Boots or bandages are worn to protect the horse's legs against injury when jumping.

APPROACH & TAKE-OFF

Approach

Take-off

Approach the jump at a controlled trot or canter, with enough **impulsion** to clear it. The horse lowers his head to judge the jump, then brings his hocks under to lift his **forehand**. He tucks up his fore legs and stretches to clear the width as he draws up his hind legs.

• HANDS
Keep your hands light – do not use them for **balance** – and encourage him to stretch his back.

POSITION •
On approach, use your back and legs. As he takes off, incline your upper body forwards.

FROM BEHIND
Lean forward to avoid being left behind or hindering the horse.

JUMPING FAULTS

Refusing to jump

Most jumping problems are caused by faulty riding or incorrect training. If a horse is badly presented at a fence, he may refuse or hit it, run out, or even fall. He will find it difficult to jump if he is unbalanced, or if he approaches too fast or too slowly. Never interfere in the final strides. If you jab his mouth to save yourself you may make him afraid of jumping. Rough hands, tension, and uncontrolled lower legs all have a negative effect. Avoid jumping too much – it will sour him; also avoid jumps that are badly built or sited.

Landing

Recovery

LANDING & RECOVERY

As the fore legs touch down, his head and neck come up. When the hind legs land, he lifts his **forehand** to get away on the landing stride. Keep your head up so you do not collapse over his neck, hindering his recovery. Sit up lightly, knees in but supple, your feet under you, reins in light contact.

LANDING POSITION •
As he lands, straighten up to reduce the weight over his fore legs. Absorb the landing impact through your ankle and knee joints, which stops your weight hitting the saddle.

• HANDS
Allow your hands to follow through, on supple shoulders and elbows, without interference to his mouth.

TAKING A LEAD
Jumping can be more difficult when leaving other horses, or going away from home. It may be easier to follow a lead. Here, pupils watch the instructor and wait their turn.

BIGGER JUMPS

A spread

To be able to clear bigger jumps, you need a well controlled, balanced approach and must be able to judge an accurate take-off point. You also have to know how to regulate **impulsion**, speed, and length of stride on the flat, and apply it to jumping.

An upright

ADVANCED RIDING

*Using finer **aids** to get the best out of your horse*

IT USUALLY TAKES MANY YEARS to become an advanced rider, and at least five years to train an advanced horse. The systematic development of a horse's ability, often called **dressage**, aims to make him more powerful, yet supple, attentive, and confident. An untrained horse carries most of his weight over his fore legs. In training, this is transferred to the hindquarters and the power of the hocks is developed. With a lightened, raised **forehand**, the horse becomes more mobile, and able to perform in perfect balance with his rider.

POSITION
The rider sits deep, but not heavy, in the saddle. He is erect but supple – not stiff.

ADVANCED PACES

A **collected** horse carries his weight, and that of his rider, evenly over all four legs. As his hocks become more **engaged**, he can contract his paces and extend them. The rider learns the **aids** to collect and **extend** the walk, and perform collected, **medium**, and **extended** trot and canter.

THE RIDER
The rider encourages the horse to stretch using educated seat, leg, and hand **aids**.

COLLECTED TROT
Above: With short, slightly elevated strides the horse springs forward energetically, with a supple back and neck, and lightened shoulders.

EXTENDED TROT
Right: Propelling himself with his hindquarters, the horse lengthens his strides to cover as much ground as possible. His frame lengthens, but he remains **on the bit**.

LATERAL WORK

Lateral work increases suppleness, obedience, and **balance**. In lateral exercises the horse is slightly bent, and his **forehand** and quarters move on different tracks. Most are performed at sitting, **collected** trot, some are done at canter, and a few at walk. Independent leg and hand **aids** are necessary.

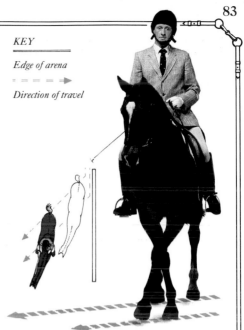

HALF-PASS
In the trot half-pass, the horse moves on a line that is diagonal to the side of the arena. The outside legs cross in front of the inside legs. The rider determines bend and direction with the inside hand and leg.

HALF-PASS FROM THE FRONT
When viewed from the front, the crossing of the fore legs is clearly seen. The forehand slightly leads the quarters. The horse **bends** in the direction of travel, the rider's outside leg and hand limiting the bend.

SHOULDER-IN
The horse is bent away from the direction of travel, at an angle of about 30 degrees to the edge of the arena. The inside fore and hind legs pass ahead of the outside fore and hind legs, making three tracks.

HAUNCHES-IN
In this movement, the **haunches** are at an angle of 30 degrees to the arena's edge. The horse **bends** in the direction he is going, and moves on three or four tracks. His outside legs pass in front of his inside legs.

TURNING ON THE SPOT

*Turn on the haunches
(demi-pirouette) at the walk*

A horse turns on the spot by pivoting around his inside hind leg (turn on the **haunches**) or inside fore leg (turn on the **forehand**). A demi-pirouette is a turn of a half circle (right) and a pirouette is a full circle. To do the pirouette at the canter requires an advanced state of collection and training.

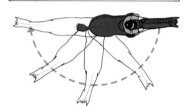

TURN ON THE HAUNCHES

Above and right: In this turn, the fore feet and outside hind foot move around the inside hind. The turn is started from a **collected** walk, or a **square halt**. The horse **bends** slightly towards the turn.

THE FLYING CHANGE

The flying change is changing the **leading** legs at the canter. It can be executed in sequence – every third stride, for example. The changes must be balanced and rhythmic.

Change

• **LEGS**
The **leading** fore and hind legs are switched during the moment of **suspension**.

Left lead

Right lead

• THE RIDER

The outside leg asks the horse to turn and holds the quarters in position. The inside leg controls the turn, maintains **impulsion**, and prevents a backwards tendency.

TURN ON THE FOREHAND

Above: The turn on the **forehand** is useful for learning leg **aids**. However, it does not require **collection** and, as the horse's weight is over the forehand, it is not regarded as an advanced exercise.

ADVANCED MOVEMENTS

Movements such as passage, piaffe, and pirouette at a canter, require the most advanced stage of **collection**. They demand lightness of **forehand**, great suppleness, and maximum **impulsion**. They are the ultimate result of developing the horse's natural paces and physique.

PASSAGE

Passage is a springy, **elevated** trot, with long moments of **suspension**, as if in slow motion. The **forehand** is raised and light, producing a perfectly balanced movement.

PIROUETTE

The horse canters a full circle on the spot, pivoting around his inside hind leg. He maintains the canter rhythm, and he must "sit" on his hocks to elevate his **forehand**.

TROUBLESHOOTING

How to cope with problems that may occur when you are riding

IF YOU HAVE CHOSEN a good riding school, you will be riding suitable, well-behaved horses, and they, and their tack, should be safe and in good condition, so few problems should occur. However, it is as well to know what to do if something does go wrong. Horses are naturally suspicious of anything strange, and their instinctive reaction when frightened is to jump away (**shy**), or take flight (bolt). They can also swing around, refuse to go forward, or try to return home (**nap**). More serious is **rearing** (standing up on the hind legs), a vice that is both dangerous and difficult to cure. A very fresh or excitable horse may present different problems. He may jog, pull, **buck**, or kick out at other horses. However frustrating your horse's behavior, try to keep calm and never resort to violence or lose your temper – it always makes matters worse. Ride positively to give him confidence, and stay alert, looking ahead to anticipate problems or hazards in advance.

PROBLEM BEHAVIOR

You may find your horse is stubborn or he may be reluctant to leave his companions, or his stable or field. If he stops, reverses, or turns around, keep a firm contact with your hands and legs, and ride him forward vigorously. A horse that persists in **napping**, **rearing**, **bucking**, or **shying**, will need an experienced rider to correct him.

NAPPING
Ride positively, with firm legs, seat, and hands, and encourage him if he hesitates with a click, or growl. He is less likely to **nap** if with a companion.

SHYING
Turn his head away from the object he dislikes, by keeping a firm hold on the outside rein. This makes him easier to control and he will find it difficult to **shy**.

REARING
Try to prevent **rearing** by riding forward strongly, in any direction. If he does rear, lean forward without pulling the reins. Avoid any horse known to rear.

TACKLING PROBLEMS

Most problems that may occur on a hack are solved by common sense. If your horse loses a shoe, lead him home, avoiding hard roads. Remove a "spread" shoe as soon as possible, without tearing his hoof, to avoid injury. Decent tack should not break, but if a rein or girth snaps, stop, dismount, and walk home.

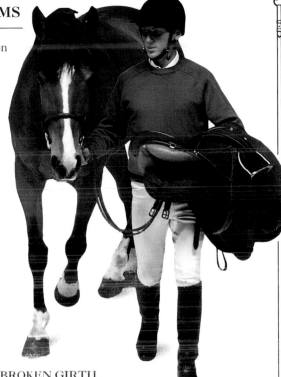

LAMENESS
Above: Running up a horse to test for soundness. If he goes lame, check his foot for stones, and his leg for soreness. Lead him home if necessary.

BROKEN GIRTH
If your girth breaks when you are moving at a fast pace you are likely to fall off. However, if you realize it is detached while you are still in the saddle, dismount very carefully, remove the saddle and carry it as you lead him back to the stable.

IF YOU FALL OFF
Most falls are preventable if you have a firm, **balanced** seat, can manage your horse, and you always plan ahead. But if you do fall, try to relax and, unless you are going fast and are likely to be dragged, hang on to the reins if possible, to prevent him getting loose.

IF A COMPANION FALLS OFF
If your companion falls, letting go of the horse, try to catch it. If she is not hurt then she may remount and continue the ride. If she is injured, send someone to get help, preferably leading the loose horse. A knowledge of first aid is always useful.

HORSE CARE

Looking after the welfare and daily needs of your horse

WHEN WE CONFINE HORSES IN STABLES we deprive them of their freedom, so we should do our best to keep them healthy and happy in this unnatural environment. Most horses are quite content if they are given a suitable diet and plenty of clean, fresh bedding in well-drained, well-ventilated stables. They thrive on routine, being happiest with regular feeding, cleaning, and exercise – so every effort must be made to provide a daily routine. If possible, they should be turned out in a field for part of the day, or at night, especially if they are not being exercised. They should be kept dry and warm in winter, and away from insects and hot sun in summer.

FEEDING

What to feed, how much, and when, depends on the horse – his size, age, whether he is stabled, and the work he does. A horse digests food slowly so feed little and often. Always let him drink before feeding, and allow him at least an hour for digestion before work. Don't feed him when he is hot and tired. Avoid sudden changes of diet.

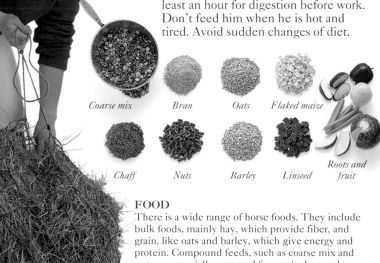

Coarse mix *Bran* *Oats* *Flaked maize*

Chaff *Nuts* *Barley* *Linseed* *Roots and fruit*

FOOD
There is a wide range of horse foods. They include bulk foods, mainly hay, which provide fiber, and grain, like oats and barley, which give energy and protein. Compound feeds, such as coarse mix and nuts, are specially prepared for particular needs. Carrots, apples, and other succulents add variety.

MUCKING OUT

The stable must be cleaned out regularly. A clean bed keeps your horse warm, encourages him to lie down, and to stale (urinate), cushions his legs, and protects him from injury.

• *Broom*

• *Four-pronged fork*

• *Shovel*

Skep •

Wheelbarrow •

Boots •

Shavings rake *Rake* *Pitchfork*

Straw *Paper* *Shavings*

EQUIPMENT
Stable yard equipment includes: a wheel-barrow; a skep for collecting droppings; forks, for lifting soiled bedding and shaking out straw; and a shovel, rake, and broom for cleaning beds of shavings or sawdust.

BEDDING
Bedding should not overheat when soiled, or harm the horse if he eats it. Straw drains well; wood shavings are less dusty and drain better than sawdust or peat. Paper is suitable for horses that are allergic to dust or spores.

1. REMOVE THE MUCK
Remove haynets and any buckets. Pick up all the visible droppings with a fork and then separate the soiled bedding from the clean, and lift it into the wheelbarrow.

2. SWEEP THE FLOOR
Pile the clean bedding in the corners or along the sides of the stable, and sweep up the remaining soiled bedding, using the broom and shovel, and leave the floor to dry.

3. REPLACE THE BED
Replace the clean bedding evenly, using a pitchfork (or rake for shavings), then top it up with a fresh layer if necessary, building it up at the sides for extra protection.

BLANKETING

Blankets are worn by stabled horses in cold weather, especially if they have a fine or clipped coat. Blankets also provide protection for horses outside. Horses that live outside grow thick coats in winter and will sweat when they are worked, so losing condition. They are often clipped to counteract this, but then need the warmth of a blanket to replace their coat.

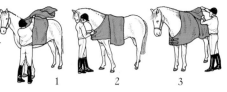

PUTTING ON A BLANKET

Throw the blanket forward over his back, or fold it in half and place it across his **withers** (1). Fasten it at the front (2), ensuring it will not chafe as he moves. Straighten it out (3). Never pull it forwards against the hair. Fasten the **roller**, or **surcingle**, and leg straps if there are any (4).

BLANKET SIZE
To find out what size blanket your horse needs, measure the distance from the front of his chest to his tail.

ROLLER
The **roller**, or **surcingle**, is padded and must not press on his spine. Fasten it tightly enough to stop it moving or slipping.

FILLET STRING
The fillet string (a length of fine cord) crosses behind the quarters and under his tail, and prevents a light blanket from blowing in the wind.

TYPES OF BLANKET

There are many types of blanket, specially designed for different purposes.

Jute blankets, lined with wool, are hard-wearing but they can be heavy, especially as they are often used with a second blanket for extra warmth. Blankets of synthetic materials are lighter than jute blankets and are easier to clean. The best ones provide excellent insulation and warmth. Day or traveling blankets vary in thickness. They are usually made of colored wool and are edged with cotton.

Weatherproof blankets, such as the New Zealand, for horses that live outside,

are usually canvas and are lined with wool. These blankets are quite bulky and heavy, and tend to rub the shoulders and **withers**, so they should have padding, and must be checked at least once a day. Leg straps, or cross-over straps, must be kept soft, clean, and supple to avoid any rubbing, which will make the horse sore.

Cotton sheets provide protection from flies and dust in hot weather. Anti-sweat blankets, usually cotton, string, or towelling, help to prevent a chill on a wet or sweating horse. Another blanket can be placed on top of them for extra warmth.

A DAY AT THE STABLES

A typical day begins early with checking the horses, straightening their blankets, and removing empty haynets. Water buckets are cleaned and refilled and food is given. After the feed, the stables are mucked out. The horses are brushed, their manes and tails tidied, and their feet picked out, ready to be tacked up.

Most horses have about 1½ hours' daily exercise. This can be either school work or hacking, or both. On their return to the stable they are untacked, and sweat marks are sponged off. If it is cold their blankets are put on; in warm weather they can be led out, before having a haynet.

Later, after a thorough grooming, they are given a midday feed. In the afternoon, droppings are picked up, haynets are refilled, and the water supply is checked. The horses are blanketed before their evening feed. A final check will be given later in the evening.

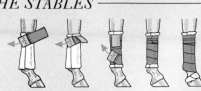

BANDAGING

Bandages protect the lower legs, between the fetlock and the knee, or hock, and should not interfere with the **flexion** of the joints. Their pressure must be even and firm, but not restrictive. The bandages should be neatly rolled up before you start. Begin at the top, on the outside, and wrap the bandage down the leg to just above the fetlock, then up again, securing the whole bandage at the top. Roll it in the same direction as the overlap on the padding, if used, to keep it flat. Stable or travel bandages continue over the fetlocks, into his heels, to keep him warm and protected.

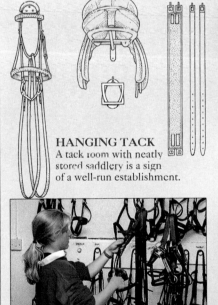

HANGING TACK
A tack room with neatly stored saddlery is a sign of a well-run establishment.

SWEEPING THE YARD
The stables and yard are kept hygienic by daily mucking out, frequent removal of droppings, and regular sweeping.

CLEANING TACK
Tack needs regular care. Always wash the bit after use, and clean the saddle and bridle, especially buckles and joins.

MUCKING OUT THE FIELD
Grassland soon becomes horse-sick if it is over-grazed. Droppings are removed regularly, to avoid worm-infestation.

GLOSSARY

Words in *italics* are glossary entries.

A

•**Above the bit** The horse evading *contact* by carrying his head too high.
•**Action** The way the horse moves.
•**Advanced** A horse, or rider, with highly developed training.
•**Aids** Signals a rider uses to convey his intentions to his horse.

B

•**Balance** The distribution of weight between horse and rider.
•**Bars** Toothless gums in the horse's mouth. As they have the most feeling the bit is positioned to rest on them.
•**Behind the bit** The horse evading rein *contact* by bringing his head in close to his chest.
•**Bend** The arc formed by the horse's body as he turns to the left or to the right.
•**Between leg and hand** Keeping the horse attentive to both hand and leg *aids*, balanced and ready to do what the rider asks.
•**Bucking** (Buck) The horse leaping in the air, with an arched back and head held low, without being asked.

Above the bit

C

•**Changing the rein** Changing the direction of travel around an arena or school.
•**Collected** (Collection) When a horse's hind legs are brought well under his body, raising his *forehand* and appearing to shorten his outline.
•**Conformation** The physical structure of the horse.
•**Contact** The link, made through the reins, between horse's mouth and rider's hands.
•**Curb** A chain attached to some bits that acts on the chin groove.

D

•**Dressage** The systematic training of the horse to develop his physical ability and obedience.

E

•**Elevated** When the horse lifts his legs higher than normal.
•**Engaged** The hind legs being brought well under his body.
•**Extended** Stride being lengthened at walk, trot, or canter.

F

•**Flexion** (Flex) Bending the neck in response to *aids*. Lateral flexion is when the horse is trained to bend his body with suppled muscles.
•**Forehand** Front of the horse, i.e. the head, neck, *withers*, shoulders, and fore legs.
•**Forward seat** Riding position for jumping or galloping when the rider's weight is moved forward over the center of balance.

G

•**Girth galls** Sores caused by an ill-fitting, hard, or dirty girth, especially when the horse is soft or unfit.

•**Grakle noseband** Noseband in two parts, crossed in a figure of eight and fastened both above and below the bit, to discourage bit evasion or prevent him crossing his jaw.

H

•**Haunches** The hips and buttocks.
•**Horsemanship** Looking after the horse in every respect.

I

•**Impulsion** Energy that is produced by the horse's hindquarters.
•**Independent seat** The ability to maintain a firm, balanced position without depending on the reins.

L

•**Lead** (Leading) The leg that reaches further forward at the canter. In canter to the right, the off fore and off hind should lead; in canter to the left, the near fore and near hind should lead.
•**Leg-yielding** The action of moving the horse sideways, away from the inside leg.
•**Loose box** An enclosed area or stable where a horse is kept.

M

•**Medium** Paces of medium length, between *working* and *extended*.
•**Mounting block** Low block of steps, or similar, for raising the rider nearer the stirrup when mounting.

N

•**Nappy** When a horse is stubborn refusing to go where asked.
•**Near side** Left side of the horse.
•**Neckstrap** A strap around the horse's neck used for extra safety when learning to ride.

O

•**Off side** Right side of the horse.
•**On the bit** The horse moving with *balance* and *impulsion* and showing no resistance to the *aids*.

P

•**Posting** (Post) Alternately rising and sitting to the rhythm of the trot.

R

•**Rearing** Rising up on the hind legs without being asked to do so.
•**Roller** A girth with padding on either side of the *withers*.

S

•**Saddle sores** Sores caused by an ill-fitting or dirty saddle.
•**Shying** (Shy) Swerving sideways away from an object or noise.
•**Square halt** The horse standing with equal weight on all four legs.
•**Stirrup lights** Battery-operated lights that attach to the stirrups.
•**Strike-off** The first step of a canter.
•**Surcingle** Narrow belt that keeps a blanket or saddle in place.
•**Suspension** When all four legs are off the ground.

T

•**Transition** The movement and moment of a change of pace, e.g. from trot to canter.

W

•**Withers** The base of the horse's neck where it joins the body.
•**Working** Average, active paces between *collected* and *medium*.

Behind the bit

INDEX

ACKNOWLEDGMENTS

Dorling Kindersley would like to thank the following for their help in the preparation of this book:
Snowball Farm and Mrs Western-Kaye for indoor and location facilities, and Rachel Hunt for additional location facilities. Mr Compton of Calcutt & Sons, Sutton Scotney for tack and clothing, Olympus Sport for tracksuits and trainers, and Rosalind Cecil for paper bedding. Mr Ricketts of Carlton Horse Transport. Also thanks to Jackie Hoadley.
The models, both human and animal. They are:
Pauline Jones on Jaffa, owned by Mrs Bonner; Barry Shaw on Toyboy, owned by Anastasia Alexander; Tim Pearson on Wait and See, owned by Mrs Hall; Rachel Hunt on Matinée, her own horse; Sarah Anne Alflatt on Tonto, owned by Nathalie Western-Kaye; Nathalie Western-Kaye on Ethel, owned by Robin Wight; Alexis, Fizz and Tiny, owned by Mrs Western-Kaye; Anna Crass-Lewis on Mattie, owned by Rosalind Daniels; Melanie Roughan; and Karey Baker.
Mary Gordon Watson rode Redstone Hill, owned by Rachel Hunt.

Additional photography by:
Bob Langrish pp.2, 6-7, 10-11, 16(br), 18(bl), 19(b), 22(bl), 63(t), 70(b), 74(b), 75(tr,b), 79(r), 80(tl), 81(b), 83(tl), 85(b), 86(bc,br), 87(c,b), 89(b), 91.
Tim Ridley pp.16(bl), 88, 89(t). Stephen Oliver pp.9(tr), 11(bl).
Kit Houghton p.86(bl).

Full-colour illustration pp.18-19 by Nicholas Hall. Other artwork by Janos Marffy, Bill Payne, Coral Mula, Jim Robins, Pete Serjeant, John Woodcock. Additional editorial assistance Deborah Opoczynska, Laurence Henderson, and Diana Weeks Index Hilary Bird.

Proof reading Heather Dewhurst. Checking Anna Buxton and Ann Kay. Make-up by Jenny Jordan. Photographic help Bob Gerrish, Debbie Sandersley, Studio Workshop. Thanks to The Cooling Brown Partnership.